The seven steps of effective EXECUTIVE COACHING

Sabine Dembkowski, Fiona Eldridge and Ian Hunter

Foreword by Sir John Whitmore

Viva Books Private Limited
New Delhi • Mumbai • Chennai • Kolkata • Bangalore • Hyderabad

First Indian Edition 2007

VIVA BOOKS PRIVATE LIMITED

- 4737/23 Ansari Road, Daryaganj, New Delhi 110 002
  E-mail: vivadelhi@vivagroupindia.net, Tel. 42242200
- Plot No. 76, Service Industries, Shirvane, Sector 1, Nerul, Navi Mumbai 400 706
  E-mail: vivamumbai@vivagroupindia.net, Tel. 27721273, 27721274
- Jamals Fazal Chambers, 26 Greams Road, Chennai 600 006
  E-mail: vivachennai@vivagroupindia.net, Tel. 28290304, 28294241
- B-103, Jindal Towers, 21/1A/3 Darga Road, Kolkata 700 017
  E-mail: vivakolkata@vivagroupindia.net, Tel. 22836381, 22816713
- 7, Sovereign Park Apartments, 56-58, K. R. Road, Basavanagudi, Bangalore 560 004
  E-mail: vivabangalore@vivagroupindia.net, Tel. 26607409, 26607410
- 101-102 Mughal Marc Apartments, 3-4-637 to 641, Narayanguda, Hyderabad 500 029
  E-mail: vivahyderabad@vivagroupindia.net, Tel. 27564481, 27564482

Published by arrangement with

Thorogood Publishers Limited
10-12 Rivington Street
London EC2A 3DU,
UK

ISBN 81-309-0507-8

Published by Vinod Vasishtha for Viva Books Private Limited, 4737/23 Ansari Road, Daryaganj, New Delhi 110 002.

Printed by Sanat Printers, Kundli - 131028.

Contents

PART TWO
The seven core capabilities of effective executive coaching

THREE

FOUR

PART THREE

The Achieve Coaching Model® – the systematic approach to effective executive coaching

TWELVE

THIRTEEN

FOURTEEN

FIFTEEN

SIXTEEN

PART FOUR
Using the Achieve Coaching Model® in context

Foreword

Sir John Whitmore

It is hard to define the origins of coaching by a date or an event, but it is rooted in humanistic psychology (1960s). Its first application in the performance context was articulated by Tim Gallwey in *The Inner Game of Tennis* (1975). At about the same time in the United States, life coaching supplanted the popularity of psychoanalysts and psychics. Shortly thereafter Tim, others and I took coaching into business in the States and in Europe.

After a slow start, in the past decade or so, workplace coaching has spread like wildfire throughout the so-called industrialized world. This reflects changing social values and, in particular, the shift from dependence on external authority to the emergence of internal or self-responsibility. This is an important stage both in psycho-social evolution, and in management practice.

Naturally its applications in the workplace are many, ranging from the adoption by managers of devolved responsibility culture to the use of external coaches by executives for their career or personal development. Coaching is now a profession in its own right and as such it is formulating a set of standards and qualifications by which its practitioners can be regulated and adjudged.

There are some books that really make a contribution to the body of knowledge of the subject. This book is one of those. It is objective and research based while also drawing on the experiences of the authors and others in such a way that is not boringly academic at all. It grabs one's interest and holds it with very clear readable language.

The content is comprehensive and the book is well sequentially structured. While rooted in the experience of practitioners, it draws upon a range of methodologies and developmental models devised by different authors for support and to produce a very convincing authoritative document that will be invaluable to many coaches wishing to refine their skills. For example there are great sections on developing rapport and on good listening as well as on the harder stuff such as the structure of questions and on goal setting. The core of the book is around what the authors call the Achieve Coaching Model®, a seven stage elaboration of the widely used GROW model. I hope this will serve to downgrade GROW, not because there is anything wrong with the GROW sequence for asking coaching questions – far from it.

Unfortunately, however, the memorable nature of the mnemonic GROW and its association with coaching has obscured, or even replaced, in too many minds the real principles of coaching, that of building the Awareness and the Responsibility of the coachee. This model and the whole book will help to restore the priorities.

HR professionals and their companies are faced with more and more coaching offerings and find it harder and harder to choose between them. Accreditation is spreading and the criteria becoming more consistent but that alone does not tell them who to choose. This book will be of great help to those who want to know what to expect and what to look for in a coach.

So where is coaching going from here? The authors refer to this in their last chapter, Future trends and outlook. The authors keep our feet on the ground throughout the book by focusing principally on the rational processes of the mind that fulfils most corporate coaching needs, but we should not forget that much of what drives us is subconscious. The subconscious mind is often easier to access through non-linear techniques such as imagery and free drawing. Also a wellspring of untapped potential lies in the higher mind, sometimes known as the super-conscious and this is where conventional coaching reveals its limitations.

As I wrote earlier, coaching was born in the cradle of humanistic psychology but it is coming of age in the next wave, transpersonal psychology, which is already influencing coaching, and the way it is taught in some accredited programmes. The authors allude to the transpersonal in an excellent chapter, Intuition and presence, both of which are transpersonal qualities that can be developed using transpersonal coaching techniques. However, it is the area where psychological and spiritual development merge and for those who struggle with the spiritual, which includes a fair share of business people, it is a no-go area before they are ready. I expect we will see more of it in the authors' next book. Meanwhile I hope you get as much out of this one as I did.

Acknowledgements

This book is the result of literally thousands of hours of listening and learning from leaders in organizations, our clients and colleagues. We are grateful for the wealth of experience and the opportunity to learn from so many people from such rich and varied backgrounds.

In particular we would especially like to thank our clients who provide us with insights and inspiration. We are also indebted to our colleagues who kindly participated in the research for this book and provided access to their knowledge, thoughts and ideas.

The following people deserve a special mention for their inspiration, input and invaluable comments on the manuscript:

- Mircea Albeanu, Orion Partners
- Prof. David Clutterbuck, Sheffield Hallam University
- Karen Drury, fe_3 Consulting
- Prof. Dr. Hans Eberspächer, Mentalinform
- Wendy Johnson, President and CEO, Worldwide Association of Business Coaches
- Prof. David Lane, Middlesex University
- Konrad Lenniger, International Top Executive Coach
- Prof. Ronald E. Riggio, Kravis Leadership Institute, Claremont McKenna College
- Neill Ross, Thorogood
- Angela Spall, Thorogood
- Sir John Whitmore, Performance Consultants
- Nick Williams, Heart at Work

Any remaining omissions, confusions or errors are, of course, our own.

PART ONE
Overview and introduction

CHAPTER ONE Introduction

ONE Introduction

We write as practitioners for practitioners. Our aim, in this book, is to contribute to the coaching profession and provide you with a pragmatic approach which achieves sustainable and measurable results for clients.

The book is for:

- coaches, trainers and consultants who want to develop their executive coaching skills and become effective executive coaches
- business leaders and managers who wish to learn about coaching and incorporate the lessons into their leadership and managerial practices
- executives responsible for buying executive coaching services and for establishing a coaching culture who wish to understand more about:
  - what to look for when comparing providers
  - how to establish a systematic approach to make internal coaching practices more efficient and how to achieve a greater return on their coaching investment
- executives who are thinking about using executive coaching services for personal and professional development and want to know more about what to expect during the coaching experience

Executive coaching is a key tool for developing managers in successful organizations. Only those individuals who behave authentically can be successful in the long term. Processes and procedures are important but without the right people working in an effective and efficient manner any organization will flounder.

Two of us have had successful careers as international management consultants with globally recognized firms and the other was a company chairman guiding the development of an organization from successful start-up to one of the top three in its sector.

When we started our international executive coaching practice, The Coaching Centre, we initiated an international best practice study. Over the course of two years we reviewed the leading literature from Europe and North America, analyzed video tapes, transcripts and material, observed coaching demonstrations and conducted in-depth interviews with leading executive coaches as well as their clients.

As a result of this research we identified seven core coaching capabilities and a seven-step process for structuring an executive coaching programme. The use of these seven steps seemed to generate significant results for coaching clients. Through our work as executive coaches we refined our systematic approach which has now been tried and tested in blue chip organizations across different industries and countries.

Our distinctive approach consists of a model that makes the key steps of executive coaching transparent. It provides the foundations upon which you can build as you develop skill and experience in the art and science of executive coaching.

The idea for this book grew from our pursuit of answers to two seemingly simple yet compelling questions:

- How do executive coaches achieve tangible outcomes for their clients?
- What is it that really makes the difference in becoming an effective and experienced executive coach?

In this book we reveal our insights from our international executive coaching practice and make the tools and techniques that make the difference between being a good and being an excellent coach transparent.

It is our conviction that transparency increases trust. It is the essential component of any coaching relationship. By being open and clear about what we think works and what does not, we aim to build your confidence so that you can be open with your coaching clients about what you are doing during coaching sessions, and why. Without trust the client holds back and does not reap the full benefits of the coaching relationship.

Trust, however, is not only the critical component of a coaching relationship. It is also vital for the future development of the coaching profession. As executive coaching continues to be in the spotlight it is recognized that there are great variations in practice and that there is a lack of consistent professional standards applied across executive coaching assignments.

Too much of what constitutes executive coaching practice remains a 'mystical art', jealously guarded by many of those who practice as executive coaches. This can force new inexperienced executive coaches into taking risks with clients by 'learning by doing' what works and what does not. The tools and techniques of executive coaching have been well described but the ways of putting it all together for effective practice are obscured. Our belief in the necessity of greater transparency fuelled our desire to 'demystify' executive coaching by shedding some light into the 'black box' of real life coaching assignments and by doing this to contribute to the further development of the discipline and professional practice.

How to use this book

The book can be read chapter by chapter or by dipping into those sections which are of immediate interest to you. Whatever method you choose, reading a book is no substitute for hands-on practical experience in executive coaching, be it as a coach or a client. Reading this book may be likened to reading a menu in a restaurant. By just reading the menu your appetite will not be sated! To have the full experience you need to read, select and then eat.

The book is organized into seven main areas:

1. **What is executive coaching?** Here we provide a definition for executive coaching and detail the key elements of the definition. We also look into the macro economic and social factors that contributed to the growth and popularity of executive coaching.
2. **The seven core capabilities of executive coaching.** The seven core capabilities are: rapport building, deep listening, creative questioning, clear goal setting, giving feedback, intuition and presence. In this chapter we describe each of these core capabilities and detail how these are used within a coaching assignment.
3. **The Achieve Coaching Model®** – the systematic approach to executive coaching. The results of our study of effective executive coaching suggest that experienced executive coaches, although flexible and interactive, follow a structured systematic approach. We identified a seven step process that forms the foundation of the Achieve Coaching Model®. Initially we experimented with the insights in our international executive coaching practice. The systematic approach has proved to produce tangible results with blue chip organizations across different industries and countries.

In this chapter we provide a detailed description of each of the seven stages, describe best practice and behaviours of successful, 'experienced' executive coaches, provide a client perspective of each stage, give top tips of experienced executive coaches and provide case studies (using pseudonyms) to illustrate the use of the model in practice.

4. **The seven core capabilities in the context of the Achieve Coaching Model®**. The critical core capabilities are described in the context of each stage of the Achieve Coaching Model® to provide practical guidance about how to use them in coaching assignments.
5. **Measuring the effectiveness of executive coaching**. Those who invest in coaching are increasingly challenged to justify their spend and provide assessments of the impact and effectiveness of the coaching programmes. As the benefits of executive coaching have tangible as well as intangible elements, there are a number of different tools and methods, including calculating the financial Return on Investment (ROI) in coaching that can be used, although there are challenges to any evaluation approach. In this chapter we provide insights into how various types of effectiveness can be assessed and explore in some depth how to use a ROI approach to measuring effectiveness.
6. **Trends and outlook**. Executive coaching as a discipline is still in its infancy. Here we share with you our perception of the current key trends in the field of executive coaching.
7. **Further reading and training**. Here you can find a list of books that inspired us and that may also stimulate your interest. For those who want to embark on an executive coach training programme we provide contact details.

We encourage you to try things out and play with the systematic process, the methods and tools we outline. Some will suit you, others will not. At the end we hope that we will have encouraged you to structure your coaching assignments whilst keeping an appetite for 'something new' to add to your toolkit and achieve great results.

Note on use of gender pronouns

Throughout the book, apart from in the case studies, we have referred to the coaching client as he. We thought hard about this before opting for a single pronoun. However, we wanted to avoid the clumsy his/her option and to alternate between he and she seemed contrived. The choice of the masculine pronoun is therefore just for convenience and consistency.

Our starting point is to define what we mean by executive coaching and to understand the evolution of coaching from the preserve of the few in the 1980s to its current position as one of the fastest growing areas of professional services.

CHAPTER TWO What is executive coaching?

TWO What is executive coaching?

Introduction

Coaching is not a new phenomenon. Many of us will have had the experience of a parent or teacher setting aside their own agenda and focusing on helping us to develop to our full potential. Coaching is something that appears to be an innate human capability and, as such, one that can be enhanced and developed to reach levels of professional excellence. At its core, coaching is a form of individual development in which the coach helps to bring out an individual's potential. The coach does this in a manner which supports, encourages and, most importantly, places responsibility for development squarely with the individual.

Our focus is on executive coaching: that is, coaching within an organizational context. Although personal matters are more often than not an integral part of the assignments, the main focus of this book is on the professional part of an executive's life.

In this chapter we provide a definition of executive coaching to ensure that we begin with a common understanding of the processes we are describing and to provide the context for the book. We also consider the factors that have influenced the growth of executive coaching as a profession, and the influences that have led to an increasing acceptance and demand for executive coaching services.

What is executive coaching?

There are many definitions of coaching (see Appendix 1) – the fact that there is such a multiplicity perhaps serves to indicate an emerging profession with, as yet, no commonly agreed core of standards and competencies. Executive coaching is a complex interpersonal interaction which is difficult to define definitively. However, there is a need for both purchasers and providers of executive coaching services to understand what is on offer and what the process aims to achieve.

In our practice, and in this book, we work with the following definition:

Executive coaching is the art and science of facilitating the personal and professional development, learning and performance of an executive by expanding his options for behaving authentically.

To clarify what is meant by our definition we have taken each of the major elements and explained them in more detail below.

Art and science: Executive coaching is a discipline that is developing. Research is underway in leading organizations and business schools to provide the theoretical underpinning of future practices for this professional service offering. The process and the techniques used in executive coaching are drawn from a wide range of research-based disciplines giving it a firm academic background. However, the practice of executive coaching requires the coach to select and use the techniques in a blend most suited to the client seated in front of them. In this sense, executive coaching is an art – where the skill, flexibility and experience of the individual executive coach and his interpretation of the methodology and situation all contribute to the success of the coaching programme.

Executive coaching is more than just an 'artful' conversation. Some may believe that simply being 'good with people' and 'easy to talk to' are all that is required to launch a successful executive coaching career. However, the capabilities, skills, breadth and depth of experiences of the executive coach as well as methodology and tools used should not be underestimated. On the other hand, simply applying 'scientifically proven' practices does not ensure achievement of the desired results. An executive coach needs to be both artist and scientist.

Facilitating: Facilitation is a non-directive form of development with a focus on guiding the executive through a process rather than simply providing advice and/or instruction.

Development, learning and performance: We use these terms to emphasize that executive coaching is an action-based activity which leads to improvement of one or more aspects of professional/personal life for the client. Executive coaching is not directionless conversation; it is always based on the achievement of specific outcomes.

Expanding options for behaving: The aim of any executive coaching programme, and indeed any personal development activity, is to increase choice for the individual client. With increased choices the client has more ways to achieve the desired goals, which ultimately means a greater likelihood of a successful outcome. With only a limited range of options any barriers that present themselves are likely to halt or delay progress towards the goal. The emphasis is on behaviour – that is, the way someone does something, rather than personality. Executive coaching operates from a belief that those who come to coaching are psychologically whole and able to benefit from the process. Executive coaching is not a substitute for psychotherapy.

Having discussed what executive coaching is, it is also important to consider the nature of the executive coaching relationship. Executive coaching takes place within an organizational context where there are partners involved other than the coach and the individual. The primary relationship is, of course, between coach and individual. However, the organization also has a stake in the relationship.

This triangular relationship needs to be carefully managed. From our experience, and from our research study, it is clear that the triangle can best be managed when each party involved fully understands their specific role and responsibilities. It is of central importance that the individual client accepts and acknowledges responsibility for the process.

It is also important to have transparency about the management of the triangle, which is why in our own coaching practice we make a specific point in all first meetings with a new client organization to discuss the roles and responsibilities of each party in greater detail.

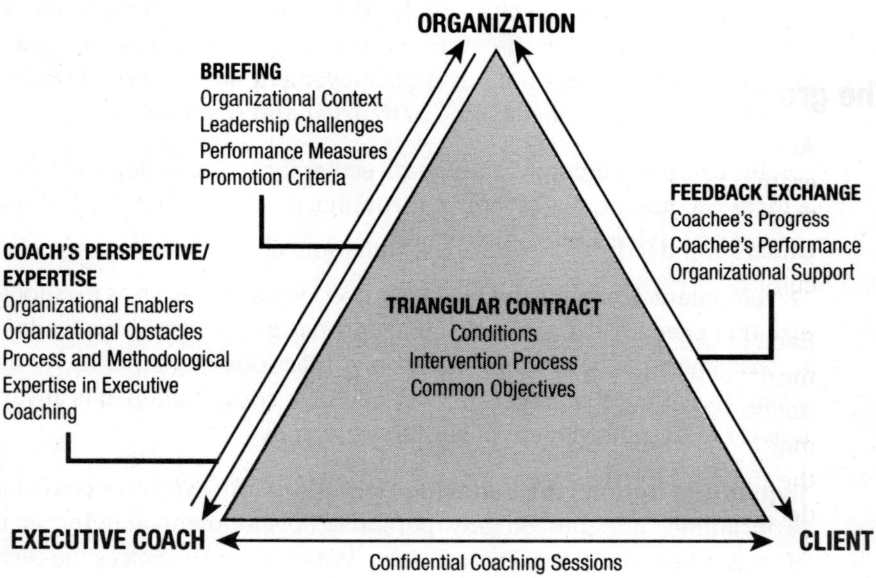

Figure 1: Partners in executive coaching

Source: Adapted from Rosinski, P. (2003), Coaching Across Cultures, Nicholas Brealey Publishing

There is now ample evidence that executive coaching is a management tool that can have a powerful sustainable impact on personal and professional development. In fact a recent study in the UK showed that more than 95% of participants who took part in a coaching assignment found the process of value[1].

The good news is that executive coaching works and generates value. The bad news is that there are great variations in the service offerings of executive coaching providers and the maximum value can only be generated by those that are well trained, have the experience to apply a systematic process and are able to draw from a great wealth of methods and techniques. It is here where we aim to add value to executive coaches, managers, organizations and executives thinking about embarking on a coaching programme.

A well-executed systematic coaching process offers executives 'just in time' (JIT) concrete, practical and relevant assistance. The JIT nature of the intervention is one of the reasons behind the growth of coaching but there are many others which have contributed to the rapid rise in popularity of coaching over the last decade. In the next section we examine some of the factors which have contributed to the rise in popularity of executive coaching to explain the climate in which coaching is used in the 21st century.

The growth of executive coaching

Across the world there is a growth in interest in coaching and a proliferation of training schools and organizations for coaching. A search on the internet produces more than 20,000 results for coach training schools. Underlying the growth of the coaching industry worldwide are social, cultural, organizational and economic factors.

Each of the factors represented in the chart below has contributed to the growth of executive coaching. Of course, for any individual or organization that turns to executive coaching the factors influencing the decision may include some, all or none of the above. Broadly, however, they are the major drivers and, in our experience, at least one influences the decision to enter a coaching relationship.

Footnote: 1 CIPD (2004): Coaching and buying coaching services.

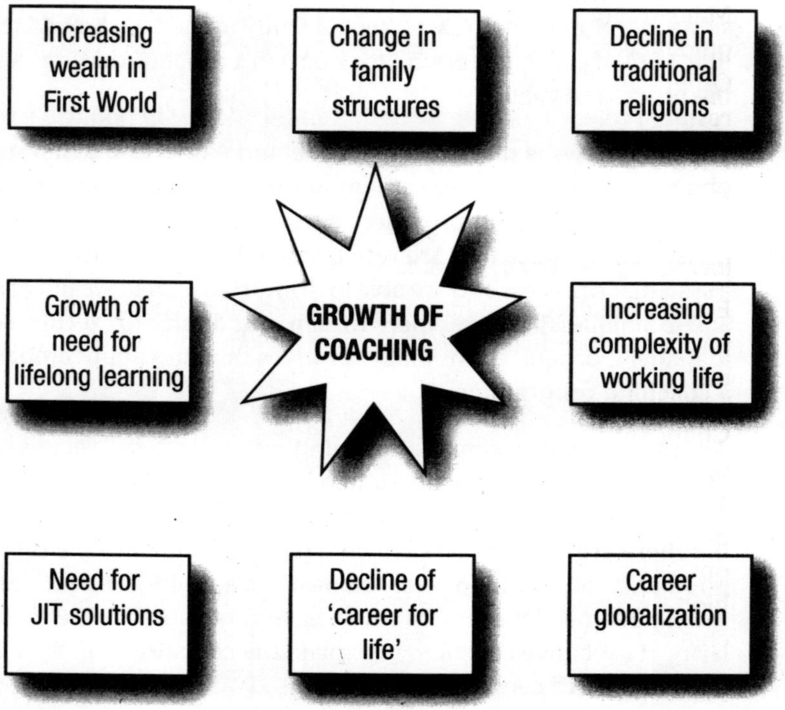

Figure 2: Growth of executive coaching: the eight critical factors

Increasing wealth in the First World

Increases in disposable income have led to many individuals in the First World being able to afford to embark on a quest to understand themselves in greater depth and develop their full potential. To achieve this they are seeking additional outside support and resources.

Change in family structures

The typical nuclear family structure is increasingly a model from the past. In many countries in Europe divorce rates are around the 50% mark. Inevitably, traditional family support structures are eroding. As a consequence people turn to others outside of their immediate family circle for support.

Decline in traditional religions

Mainstream religion used to provide another source of support and guidance. Many people now do not include religion in their daily lives. Others are finding support and guidance in alternative religions as a result of celebrity influence or driven by interest in political issues such as environmental damage. The impact of these changes has led to a greater acceptance of alternative sources of support and guidance.

Increasing complexity of working life

Even if the executive had a good personal support system, the sheer pace of change in organizations and the enormous complexity of executive roles would challenge any helpful 'amateur'.

Changes in organizational structure leading to leaner, less hierarchical operations have left some executives feeling overwhelmed by responsibilities without having clearly defined roles. Without the option of relying on formal reporting relationships and organizational support systems one client has described to us that he feels like he is, "walking on the high wire without a safety net". This has led him and others to welcome challenge and support from someone external to the organization.

Flatter structures also mean that, on promotion, individuals often have to make large changes in personal skills, performance and responsibility. With little time to settle into a new role, well executed executive coaching can help the individual make the necessary changes. In addition, there is a perceived deficit of integrity in the modern business world which has made job security and company loyalty a thing of the past. This uncertainty contributed to increasing pressure on executives to work long hours and achieve even greater results in less time. Working with an executive coach provides a 'sanctuary' for many where they can talk about issues without fear of breach of confidentiality or censure for perceived weakness. The specific knowledge of executive coaches combined with solid personal networks and well-honed soft skills are now recognized as the most important resources in the market place.

Career globalization

For many executives it is a fact of life that they will be on the move. Some change permanent locations every two years and many more travel extensively as part of their role. This can contribute to a further decline in the social network of family and real friends.

Decline of 'career for life'

The loss of 'careers for life' provides a great source of stress and uncertainty for people. It is by no means certain that a university degree or even an MBA from a well regarded business school will be the entry and insurance for a secure and rapidly progressing executive career. People now recognize that they have to assume responsibility for their own individual development rather than relying on organizational support. On average, people change career at least three times in their lives and work for five different organizations. At each career transition point executives have to prove themselves.

Need for 'just in time' (JIT) solutions

Executive coaching offers JIT learning as at its core are conversations about specific situations of an executive's life. This is in sharp contrast to the 'just in case' methods of traditional classroom based executive education programmes. In traditional training situations methods and techniques are taught and executives have to take responsibility to hoard information just in case they encounter a situation one day where the information and/or theory may become useful.

Growth of need for lifelong learning

Executives are required to learn throughout their lives to keep abreast of changing situations and to acquire new knowledge. Executive coaching is more flexible than traditional classroom based solutions and can be tailored to meet specific individual needs.

Many, if not all, of these factors contribute to an increased sense of isolation and anxiety. Executives are turning to executive coaching to help them achieve their career ambitions but also to help them to add connection and create meaning to their lives.

In the next chapter we focus on the core capabilities which provide the foundation for success in executive coaching practice.

SUMMARY: WHAT IS EXECUTIVE COACHING?

Executive coaching is the art and science of facilitating the personal and professional development, learning and performance of an executive by expanding his options for behaving authentically.

This book is built on field research that identified seven core coaching capabilities and a systematic seven-step process for structuring a coaching programme that will generate significant results.

This book provides the foundations upon which you can develop your skills and experience as a valued executive coach.

The eight factors contributing to the growth of coaching are:

- increasing wealth in the First World
- changes in family structures
- decline in traditional religions
- growth of need for lifelong learning
- increasing complexity of working life
- need for JIT solutions
- decline of a career for life
- career globalization

Many, if not all, of these factors contribute to an increased sense of isolation and anxiety. Executives are turning to executive coaching to help them achieve their career ambitions but also to help them to add connection and create meaning to their lives.

PART TWO

The seven core capabilities of effective executive coaching

Introduction

The results of executive coaching can be attributed to the careful use and orchestration of seven core capabilities. Within an executive coaching conversation all capabilities come into play. It is the orchestration of all of these core capabilities, their intensity and simultaneous play that distinguish an executive coaching conversation from a normal office conversation between colleagues. In this part of the book we provide a detailed description of the seven core capabilities of an executive coach. The seven core capabilities of executive coaching are:

- Rapport building
- Deep listening
- Creative questioning
- Giving effective feedback
- Clear goal setting
- Intuition
- Presence

CHAPTER THREE Rapport building

THREE Rapport building

Introduction

Have you ever noticed how some people are so much easier to talk to than others? Maybe you are one of those people yourself and that is what sparked your interest in developing your executive coaching capabilities. But is this something which is just innate or can it be developed?

The good news is that this is the fundamental building block of all human interactions and a skill which we all naturally have to some extent. True, some people are better at it than others but as a skill it is something which we can build upon and practise. So, would it be useful to an executive coach to be able to easily and confidently talk to others and to give others the ease and confidence to talk to them? Absolutely, without this ability the coaching relationship will flounder at the first hurdle. In fact, it may not go beyond the initial 'get to know' each other meeting.

Experienced executive coaches are typically warm, attentive, and easy to talk and relate to. These executive coaches have honed their skills so that they can work with their clients to develop a good rapport.

In developing their rapport skills, executive coaches need to be able to understand:

- What is rapport?
- How is rapport created?
- How to achieve greater rapport

What is rapport?

Rapport is the essence of close cooperation in communication between people. It is often described as a feeling of warmth and trust leading to a sense of relatedness and connection. Rapport is an interactive phenomenon that cannot be created by one person alone. It requires the cooperation of both parties and forms the foundation of any coaching conversation.

In seeking to understand what rapport is, it is useful to think about a situation where rapport was missing. As you reflect upon that now, what was it about that interaction that lead you to know that there was no rapport? Perhaps the other person was using words that were unfamiliar, technical language or acronyms specific to a particular workplace or perhaps they were wearing very different clothes. Maybe they were talking very quickly and loudly, and you prefer to speak slowly and quietly. You might even have felt a chill on meeting them. These elements and others, which we will explore next, all impact on rapport.

How is rapport created?

It is a basic human characteristic to like people who are like us. We tend to show our affiliations with others by becoming similar to them. This can be on a highly visible and conscious level such as the shared clothing styles of a gang or an organization or on a more unconscious level of the shared gestures of a couple in love. In fact scientists found that some intense dislikes such as, for example, a spider phobia may be caused because the object of fear is so different in appearance from us.

The key elements in building rapport are:

- physical appearance
- body language and gestures
- voice qualities
- language/words

Physical appearance

The closer we resemble each other the greater the feeling of comfort that is generated. Actual physical resemblance is often cited as an important factor in choosing a life partner. Obviously, in an executive coaching relationship we are not seeking such a close connection but we do want to lessen any barriers to effective communication. This means that the executive coach needs to consider such elements as, for example, style of dress.

It seems that observation of external superficial similarities generates a subconscious tendency to conclude that the other person is indeed 'like us'. This, in turn, leads to an increase of trust and hence a more solid foundation for conversation.

For an executive coach working in the business world it is therefore important to pay attention to the styles and symbols adopted by potential clients. What is the dress code? Will your disposable pen be appropriate? On one level these considerations may seem frivolous but the executive's decision about whether or not to use your service will depend on the signals you send about your ability to operate at his level.

Body language

One of the key indicators of good rapport between people is their use of shared posture and gestures. Just watch any couple in love. Their gestures and movements match each other. It is almost like a dance: one leans forward, then the other; one brushes back hair, so does the other.

These are very obvious signs, but rapport can be built more subtly as well through such things as breathing or even blinking at the same pace. For executive coaches it is useful to build observational skills so that they notice not only the more obvious elements of body language but also the subtleties.

A note of caution – be wary of attributing meaning to movements and gestures. We cannot be certain of the meaning – all sorts of factors including cultural differences will influence meaning – but we can notice changes and hence the impact we are having on our clients. Successful executive coaches will deliberately seek to enhance rapport by matching some elements of body language. For example, by adopting a more relaxed posture than normal if the client is relaxing back into the chair.

Voice qualities

Matching of the tone, speed and timbre of a voice are also indicators of a greater rapport between executive coach and client. This has even greater importance when talking on the telephone where other key elements of rapport such as body posture cannot be observed.

As an example of how an executive coach can use a combination of voice and body language matching, consider this recent session with one of our clients:

CASE STUDY: 'ROAD RAGE'

Sam came to the session following a rather lengthy and frustrating board meeting. To reach our offices he had had to drive through rush hour traffic in a thunderstorm. When he arrived he was out of breath, speaking quickly and loudly and venting his anger about fellow board members, traffic and a taxi driver who had pulled out in front of him. He did not sit down and was pacing around the room. Sabine also remained standing and kept a high energy level in her voice by speaking a little more quickly and loudly than normal when she greeted him. Although she was not sharing his anger she was matching him and created rapport by starting the session at the same energy level as Sam, whilst standing.

In the above example rapport was achieved quickly. An alternative approach where a coach could try to calm the client down by speaking slowly and softly whilst already sitting in a chair would be likely to cause dissonance and create unnecessary barriers for the start of the session.

Language/words

Although words account for only 7% of any human communication, matching the use of language and key words are important elements in deepening rapport. We probably notice this most when we get it wrong. In a work context this might result in feelings of isolation and lack of rapport when first joining a company where everyone else is using acronyms which seem like a stream of gibberish to you.

For an executive coach it is important to listen to the words that your client uses and also the way in which they use language. For example, if they say they are feeling low make sure you use the same phrase with them. If you ask them why they are sad (when low means lacking in energy to them) then you are not likely to create the optimum level of rapport.

A client's use of key words and phrases can also indicate their preferences for learning and storing information – visual, auditory or kinaesthetic (feelings – physical and emotional), olfactory and gustatory. By understanding the preferred way of making sense of the world you can then shape your communication style so that it has maximum impact. If the client tends to say things that indicate a visual preference (e.g. "I can picture that" or "I am a bit hazy about this") then you can use visual language with them. You may, if you are a person with a preference for a visual representation system, use the phrase "Is that clear?" when checking for understanding. Whereas for a client with a kinaesthetic preference you may ask "Have you got a handle on that?"

It is also important to think about the appropriateness of the language in which the coaching is delivered. For example, in international businesses it is common to use English as the main working language and clients would be used to this. However, in smaller national German companies this would not be the case and the use of English words and phrases interspersed with the native language would not be welcomed and may even be regarded as bad manners.

How to achieve greater rapport

Rapport can be increased or more easily developed by matching any of the elements described above. In the beginning this may be challenging for a new executive coach as trying to adapt to another's style can seem awkward and requires flexibility. Begin by noticing where the client differs from you. Does he have a different speed of speaking? A different body posture? A frequently used sweeping gesture?

Once you have identified these differences you can shift your behaviour towards his style. However, it is important to do this subtly. To be too overt may be seen as alienating and offensive, and many people are aware of the technique which is commonly part of communication training, especially for those with a sales background.

The key is to be similar rather than identical: you are not trying to be an exact mimic. For example, a male executive coach and a female client are likely to have different vocal ranges. The aim is for the male executive coach to raise the tone slightly not to speak in falsetto!

As an executive coach with an understanding of rapport you also bear a professional and ethical responsibility in your use of techniques to increase rapport and to determine the appropriate level. Too cosy and comfortable a relationship can lead to misunderstandings and a breakdown of the working relationship.

Before increasing rapport with the client it is important to consider why you are doing this. What is your intended outcome? For example, it is important to deepen rapport at the first meeting with a new client so that the relationship begins to be established. It is also important to achieve good rapport at the start of each session. However, it is equally important to notice when to decrease rapport. Typically this will be towards the end of a session when you are preparing to take your leave of the client. It may also be important if the client appears to be getting too emotionally close to you.

Within an executive coaching relationship it is important that there is a good working level of rapport. To illustrate this we have represented the rapport framework for executive coaching in the Figure below and provide an explanation of the five stages that may overlap.

The five rapport stages in executive coaching

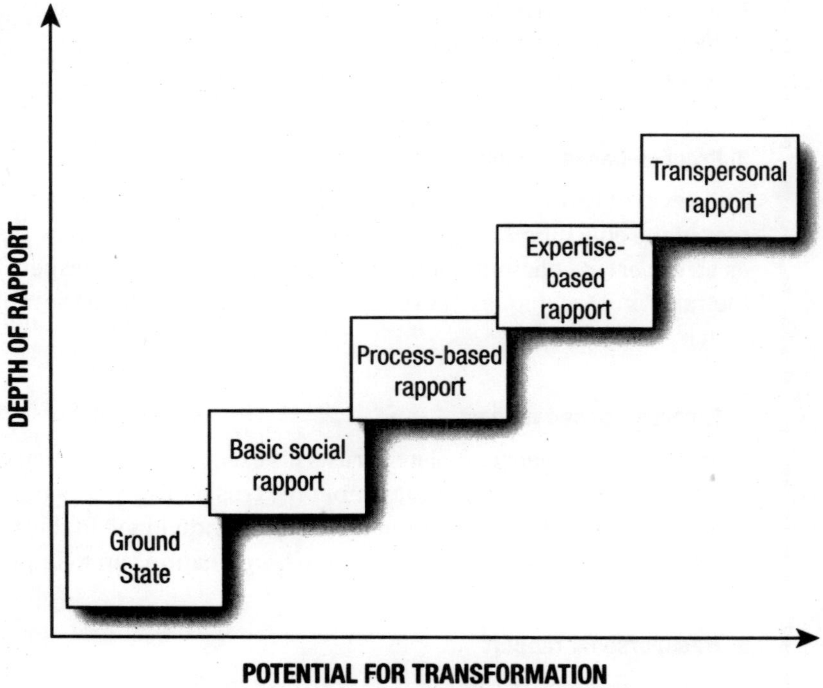

Figure 3: Rapport stages in executive coaching
Source: Adapted from M.Schmidt-Tanger (1999), Veränderungscoaching Kompentent veränderun, Junfermann

1. Ground state

This describes the position where no rapport exists between the executive coach and his client. This is typically the state when there is no relationship between the two individuals or where there has been a breakdown of the relationship. It is a state which does not provide a foundation for entering or continuing a working relationship between an executive coach and a client.

2. Basic social rapport

This type of rapport is marked by the conventions and rules of basic social politeness. Observing an executive coach and client interacting in this way it looks like a cultivated conversation where the client politely answers the questions of the executive coach. Typically this type of rapport is found in the early stages of a 'get-to-know-each-other' meeting where the executive and the executive coach meet for the first time or at the beginning of a coaching session. If the executive does not feel secure he is not likely to wish to leave this state which acts as a 'safe house'. In addition, executive coaches who are risk averse may also have no desire to leave this state. However, the ability to leave this stage distinguishes an experienced executive coach from a new executive coach.

3. Process-based rapport

This level of rapport is marked by an agreement to the general principles of the coaching process. The executive coach is viewed by the client as an expert in coaching methods. Rapport is gained via respect for the methods and techniques of executive coaching rather than the individual coach.

4. Expertise-based rapport

At this stage the client completely trusts his executive coach. Deep rapport exists between them as the client not only trusts the process but he also trusts and respects the executive coach as an individual. In this position the executive takes himself to a state where change can take place.

5. Transpersonal rapport

Achieving this type of rapport is an advanced skill. It can best be described as a situation where 1+1 = 3. In other words, the two partners in the coaching relationship act as one – akin to the way in which a champion dancing pair create a winning performance when together but are merely technical experts when dancing with alternative partners.

Something outside of the relationship carries it forward and enables the coaching experience to become transformational. The stronger the presence of this third element the more likely the coaching is to have a sustainable impact. Experienced coaches can offer this, however, it is ultimately the responsibility of the client to determine how much they are prepared to trust in the process.

The greater the depth of rapport the greater the potential for transformation and results.

SUMMARY: RAPPORT BUILDING

The ability to develop rapport with the coaching client is fundamental to the success of an executive coaching relationship.

Rapport is developed through a combination of matching:

- physical appearance
- body language and gestures
- voice qualities
- language

It is also enhanced by mutual trust and respect, and shared aims and outcomes for the executive coaching programme.

Coaches need to be able to vary the level of rapport appropriate to the needs of the client and the stage of the coaching process. There are five rapport stages in executive coaching:

1. Ground state
2. Basic social rapport
3. Process based-rapport
4. Expertise-based rapport
5. Transpersonal rapport

The greater the depth of rapport the greater the potential for transformation and real results.

At all times rapport building skills should be used with integrity. Research demonstrates that people can intuitively clearly distinguish between honest rapport and an artificial 'act'.

CHAPTER FOUR Deep listening

FOUR Deep listening

Introduction

The ability to listen well is one of the hallmarks of an experienced executive coach. However, listening is an activity which we, perhaps all too often, take for granted. It is something we have been able to do for as long as we can remember and as such, in our opinion, is a skill which is much under-rated.

How can this everyday activity be honed to an expert level? In this chapter we describe the differences between listening in everyday and executive coaching contexts. We also detail our observations of different executive coaches' approaches to listening and how listening skills can be developed.

In general, people tend to think of listening as a passive rather than active behaviour and, as a result, do not recognize the amount of effort and skill it takes to really become an expert listener.

The first step is to appreciate that listening is not the same as hearing. Hearing is one of the five ways in which we can detect changes in our internal or external environment. By hearing something we are acknowledging the reception of a sound. Listening then requires the interpretation of that sound to give it meaning and to determine the appropriate response.

Why listening is important

The benefits of listening for both the client and the executive coach are often insufficiently acknowledged or valued. Executive coaches who really listen:

- gain an understanding of people and situations
- can operate with more quality information enabling them to respond more fully and appropriately
- are less likely to become confused or entangled in conflicts

For the client, being listened to in the coaching relationship may be the only time where they really feel understood. The pressures of a busy executive life may mean that they, and those around them, rarely take time to listen and understand. The client feels valued and respected when his views, explanations and opinions are heard. In addition, the quality of the executive coach's listening can also enhance the client's own understanding and self-awareness by helping him to reflect on what he is saying and thinking.

CASE STUDY: 'THE WIRED TEAM MEETING – IS ANYONE LISTENING?'

In a recent coaching assignment we had the opportunity to witness at first hand what can happen when no one listens. We were brought in to work with a senior executive who heads up a major business unit of a large international organization. Our brief was to assist him to improve communication within his unit and with his positioning in the organization. As part of the process we observed him in various situations; one of which was a team meeting with his direct reports. The meeting room was in complete chaos when we arrived. Everyone had brought their laptops and people were clambering around the room to plug in the laptop power supplies. We had to ask if this was the right room for the meeting. Indeed it was.

Eventually, the meeting started. One person got up and presented his business results and the next steps that were to be taken. Apart from a few occasional glances at the screen no one was paying attention. The team members were too busy answering their own emails or working on reports which had to be finished. At the end of the presentation the presenter asked if the team had any questions. The only question that was asked was, "So, what do we have to do next?" Sighing with frustration the presenter then went through one of the slides again.

The lack of real listening by the team had cost them all additional time. This created further frustration and stress as they were all then late for their next appointments. All our client could say was, "Well, this is how it is around here." Needless to say one of our key interventions with the team was to work on improving listening skills and changing the set-up of their meetings.

What is listening?

In essence, listening within the coaching context requires active hearing of both what someone is saying and the way in which they are saying it. It also requires the ability to notice what is not being said. By really listening to the client the executive coach gains a real understanding of the issue under discussion. The experienced executive coach is able to see things from the client's perspective, to sense how something feels to him and to understand his frame of reference. The degree and quality of the executive coach's listening changes with the amount of focused effort that is directed towards a situation or a specific person.

In contrast, in an everyday context the listening is not as intense. In a conversation you do generally have an interest in the other person and what they are saying but your own concerns may distract you. It is quite common to pretend to listen – the cause of many a conflict between partners or work colleagues!

Even if you are listening, the truth is that the focus is not on the situation or the other person – you can drift off to another place, day dream, think about your 'to do' list or your next appointment. In between, you glance at the other person and encourage them to keep talking by nodding occasionally or using short phrases such as 'I see' or 'Uh huh'. It is easy to see that standard conversational listening where there is a mix of talking, listening, thinking and drifting off is not appropriate for generating successful outcomes of a coaching session.

Listening at the appropriate level is an activity which takes much energy and concentration. At the beginning of an executive coaching career it can seem quite exhausting to focus solely on the client for two or three hours. It is important to be able to recognize when concentration is wavering so that remedial action, such as taking a break, can be taken.

From our observations and experience of executive coaching sessions the key indicators of a breakdown of active listening include:

- spending a considerable amount of time at the beginning to 'get set up', i.e. taking stuff out of the bag, searching for a pen, pouring drinks whilst the client is already talking
- limited eye contact
- playing around with a pen, paper clip, coffee mug etc.
- looking out of the window

- a lack of response to what the client last described
- forcing the client to follow the coach's own train of thought
- interrupting the flow by an eagerness to present a solution, refer to a 'similar case' or a personal experience

Many of these observations were in sessions with new executive coaches but they can also occur with experienced executive coaches. An occasional lapse in concentration is forgivable but if the lapses are too long and/or happen too frequently it is most likely that this has a negative impact on the coaching relationship.

For example, in our interviews with clients it became clear they were able to recall precisely the situations when the executive coach was not really present. This had an impact on the level of trust in the relationship. In some cases the client cannot only lose faith in the executive coach but also the coaching process itself. Our qualitative finding is in line with a study by Lore International[2] in the US that found that 26% of clients said that their coach did not listen well and did not have the understanding to build upon their ideas in the coaching session. These findings are quite disturbing as they indicate that this most basic of capabilities is lacking in many executive coaching assignments.

However, we also observed many coaching sessions where executive coaches demonstrated a deep listening capability. The key indicators of deep listening are:

- good eye contact
- complete focus on the client
- providing space for the client to talk without interruption
- spending time to encourage the client to expand on what they are saying
- taking time to understand the situation from the perspective of the client
- reflecting content back to the client to demonstrate listening
- summarizing to signal and check understanding

In addition to these indicators, Terry Bacon, a well known US executive coach and CEO of Lore International, describes the deep level of

Footnote: 2 Bacon, T. and Spear, K.I. (2003), Adaptive Coaching: The Art and Practice of a Client Centered Approach to Performance Improvement, Davies-Black Publishing listening achieved by experienced coaches as "listening with their eyes as well as their ears". By this he means that experienced executive coaches watch their clients carefully for subtle shifts in physiology and for non-verbal signals. Observations of changes in physiology such as tightening of the facial muscles or changes in the blood flow to the skin's surface can indicate the impact on the client of what he is saying and may also be an indicator of what is not being said.

At this very deepest of levels the experienced executive coach is watching out for things that are not being said, i.e. gaps in information, as these can indicate the root of an issue which, if worked on, can bring about the greatest change for the client. The executive coach can stimulate the client to fill in the gaps by making statements such as "I notice that you are not mentioning what the impact of this change will be on your partner."

By having the deeper concern acknowledged the client feels understood and can then begin to explore previously unvoiced areas. In our own practice we have noticed that the client's habitual non-verbal gestures such as rubbing hands together or tapping a pen are often indicators of unvoiced concerns. In our opinion it is not possible, or even advisable, to attribute precise meaning to each gesture – the skill is in noticing and then asking the client for an explanation.

How to develop listening skills

Developing good listening skills is one of the key attributes of experienced executive coaches. There are three main components to the art of listening within a session:

- preparation – getting into the right state for listening
- developing and holding focus
- demonstrating to the client that you are listening

Before going into a coaching session it is very important for you to 'clear a space' so that you are ready and able to listen. Whatever has proceeded the coaching session must be put aside. We know from both our own experience and our observations of others that if you allow the argument you had that morning with your partner or the traffic hold-ups on the way to the session to encroach on your mind, then it becomes very hard to focus on the client.

Different executive coaches have different ways of achieving the necessary space to listen. Some, for example, will allow extra time so that they can read through the coaching record from the previous session to begin the process of re-immersion in the client's issue. Others may meditate before entering the coaching room or they may sit with a coffee and relax. Whatever method you use it is important that you develop the ability to put personal issues to one side and focus solely on the client and the coaching process.

The key to developing and holding focus lies in the executive coach having a genuine interest in the client, his situation and challenges. Without this the job becomes monotonous and routine, and the coaching relationship is likely to founder.

Experienced executive coaches demonstrate a keen interest in the life stories of their clients. One described it to us as "a great privilege" and another said "isn't it fascinating that the same situation can be perceived in so many different ways ...?"

We have also noted that experienced executive coaches have a sound service ethic and a desire to work with people to help them achieve the results they desire. Long periods of focused listening are challenging. It is a skill that requires concentration and practice. However, it is important to note that a coaching session is a mixture of listening, observing, questioning, giving feedback and interacting with the client, so if you notice that your focus is waning then you can switch to another activity such as asking more questions to help you to regain the necessary focus.

To demonstrate to the client that the coach is listening, experienced executive coaches use the following techniques:

- **Reflecting back from time to time and summarizing a sequence of the coaching conversation.** This ensures a shared understanding and sends a strong signal of 'I am right here with you'. It is essential that the executive coach refrains from making judgements and preconceptions as they give feedback to the client.
- **Integrating the client's own words in a question.** This is important as it shows both respect for the client's way of expressing something and also will have more impact as it is in his language. For example, if a client says "I need to take more time to relax" then a question could be "How will having more time to relax help you to achieve your goal?" This will have more impact than saying "How will taking time off help you?" This question does not use the client's

words and it assumes that to relax will mean having time away from work, whereas the client may have been referring to taking more time to relax during the working day.

- **Repeating critical words with an increased inflection.** This both signals that you have heard what the client has said and stimulates the client to further thought.
- **'Letting go'.** It is important that the coach follows the direction/agenda set by the client. This is the matter that occupies his mind. If, through listening, you develop a hunch or idea about something that might help the client, then write it down and come back to it at a later point. We noticed that when executive coaches were too quick to come in with suggestions then the client often became distracted and agitated. Not only does a forced change of direction use up a lot of the executive coach's energy, it also shows a lack of respect for the client and does not contribute to his learning and development.
- **'Playing paper-chase'.** It is particularly important in the initial stages of a coaching relationship or when discussing new issues, for the executive coach to follow the clues left by the client. By listening deeply the coach can work with the client to put together a complete picture and develop a coherent story. This will guide the client's self-discovery and help him put together an action plan that is genuinely personal to him and his agenda. In this way the learning and development activities are sustainable and owned by the client, rather than imposed by the coach telling the client what to do.

Advanced applications of listening

When an executive coach has truly mastered the art of listening it can appear that they are almost telepathic. It seems that the executive coach instinctively knows what the client is thinking and feeling, and employs questions and statements that cause the client to say things such as, "That's amazing, that's just what I was thinking." So how is this possible? Terry Bacon of Lore International puts it down to listening "with your heart as well as your head" and a detached "attunement to emotional frequencies".

In essence we are describing the ability of the executive coach to empathize with the client. This is demonstrated when the coach is able to communicate his understanding of the client back to the client.

Experienced executive coaches demonstrate empathy using the following techniques:

- **Recognizing and acknowledging the emotion.** Having identified an emotion coaches acknowledge it to their clients by using phrases such as, "... and that stresses you" and "... so you feel disempowered".
- **Checking perceptions.** Repeating back to the client what they thought they have heard using phrases like "I want to be sure I understand what you are saying. It sounds like ...", "Is part of what you are saying ...?", "What I hear you saying, if I understand you correctly is ...?" or "What I heard was ...?"
- **Hypothesizing how the executive is feeling.** Care must be exercised when using this technique as it could be perceived as being too directive or leading in a certain direction. If you are certain that you have grasped the situation correctly then statements such as, "It must be quite draining not to know exactly what is in your frame of responsibilities and what is not", can help crystallize the client's thinking.
- **Projecting how the client may or would feel if the situation were different.** Again this is a technique which should only be used if you have a good knowledge of the client and his issues. Statements such as, "You would be happier and more relaxed if you received constructive feedback", can be used to summarize the client's desire, particularly if it incorporates language that he has used previously.

However, it must be stressed that these are advanced techniques to be used with care and caution. If you do not feel certain that you have really understood the client's emotions and have doubts about the level of your emotional attunement it is best to get reassurance and check with simple questions such as:

- You seem ... Is this correct?
- You feel ... Have I understood this right? Am I summarizing this correctly?
- You appear to be ... Have I picked this up correctly? If not ... How would you describe this?

The ability to empathize with your client in a way which is helpful to them and takes them forward is a more advanced capability than it may initially seem.

Through talking to executive coaches and clients, and from our own coaching practice, we noticed how easy it is to fall prey to the phenomena of projection and transference.

By projection we mean ascribing to or perceiving in another person your own traits or qualities. In other words assuming that you know exactly what is going through the client's mind because it is similar to something that you do or would do if you were in the clients situation.

Transference is the displacement of patterns of feelings and behaviour, originally experienced with significant figures of your past experience, to individuals in the current coaching relationship. This can lead to false assumptions and predictions about the client and his current and future behaviour. It is an ever present danger even for experienced executive coaches. It is easy to slip into hearing what you want to hear, interpreting the client's situation too quickly in the light of your own value system or experience, and constructing the client's story based on your own view of the world. To guard against these dangers it is important to explore issues of projection and transference with your supervisor who can act as a neutral sparring partner with whom you can check your assumptions.

SUMMARY: LISTENING SKILLS

Listening is one of the most important skills that an executive coach needs to develop. It is also the coaching skill that can be most difficult to deploy consistently and is all too easily confused with hearing. Great executive coaches are great listeners before all else.

Listening in a coaching context requires the executive coach to concentrate both on what the client is saying, how the client is saying it and what he is not saying.

There are three main components to the art of listening:

- preparation – getting into the right state for listening
- developing and holding focus
- demonstrating to the client that you are listening

Deep listening allows the executive coach to become at one with the client so that a deep understanding of the client's situation can be gained. This enables the executive coach to guide the process and ask pertinent questions which facilitate the transformational process.

The key indicators of deep listening are:

- good eye contact
- complete focus on the client
- providing space for the client to talk without interruption
- spending time encouraging the client to expand on what they are saying
- taking time to understand the situation from the perspective of the client
- reflecting content back to the client to demonstrate listening
- summarizing to signal and check understanding

Experienced coaches use the following techniques to demonstrate that they are listening:

- reflecting back from time to time and summarizing a sequence of the coaching conversation
- integrating the clients own words in a question
- repeating critical words with increased inflection
- letting go
- playing 'paper-chase'

Advanced listening skills include:

- recognizing and acknowledging emotions
- checking perceptions
- hypothesizing how the executive is feeling
- projecting how the client may or would feel if the situation were different

CHAPTER FIVE Creative questioning

FIVE Creative questioning

Introduction

As executive coaching is essentially a structured conversational exchange between an executive coach and client, the ability to ask good questions lies at the heart of the experienced executive coach's toolkit. The difference between an everyday conversation in which both parties may ask questions of each other and a coaching conversation lies in the coach's careful use of simple questions with a specific purpose. Questions have a wide spectrum of uses, from simple data gathering to effecting personal change. The key for the executive coach is to know how and when to use each type of question and always to consider the likely effect of a question on the client. The skilful use of questioning requires the executive coach to be reflective: to think about the phrasing of a question and its intended outcome; to deliver the question and, most importantly, to notice the effect that the question has on the client. The development of good questioning abilities is therefore an iterative process involving practice, experimentation, observation and reflection.

Why is creative questioning important?

Good questioning lies at the heart of effective executive coaching because it is the single most important way in which an executive coach can have a direct impact on guiding the client towards achieving behaviour change and his goal. Through the skilful use of questions the coach can:

- compel the client to think, to examine, to look, to feel, to be engaged
- evoke clarity of thinking
- focus attention on critical behaviours/areas
- stimulate answers which are descriptive but not judgemental (to avoid a descent into self-criticism)
- check understanding

- increase the client's self-awareness
- promote the client's responsibility for using his resources and develop solutions
- challenge the client to take action and initiate change
- gain commitment
- obtain high quality feedback which is essential to the forward momentum of the coaching relationship

Before asking a question of the client, the coach must ponder, "What is my intention in asking this question?" This is why we advise against compiling a preset question catalogue. The questions must be asked in the context of the client and his specific situation. The coaching conversation needs to 'flow'. Questions prepared before the session or taken from a book may destroy the process if used in an inflexible, automated fashion.

During executive coach training it can be helpful to prepare and formulate questions so that you can practise them on your trial clients. However, the point of that exercise is to experience the impact that different forms of questions have on clients and to learn from that experience. As an executive coach becomes more experienced then the questions flow more intuitively and are guided by the interaction with the client.

Questioning techniques

Good coaching questions share three common characteristics:

- they are simple – questions which ramble on or contain sub questions can confuse the client and hinder the process
- they are asked with a specific purpose and
- they are designed to have a positive impact on the client rather than control him

At the beginning of the coaching process questions are used mainly to gather information. The executive coach is seeking a rich detailed description of the client and his current situation. The answers at this stage will provide background information, facts and begin to provide both coach and client with an awareness of how these things are affecting the client and his motivations for taking action. The most effective questions begin with words such as:

- What...?
- When...?
- Who...?
- Where...?

There are two notable omissions from this list which we would tend to use in everyday situations – why and how. The reasons that they are missing from the list, and why we would advise their use with caution, is because of the effect 'why' and 'how' questions have on the client. Both types of questions often seem to carry an implied criticism and can evoke defensiveness in the client. If you think back to the times you have been asked "Why....?" at school or by your parents it is probably easy to remember feelings of being reprimanded. In addition, these questions encourage analysis and justification rather than open exploration. Rather than "Why..?" the question may be rephrased as "What was your motivation...?" and "How...?" can be expressed as "What were/are the steps...?"

Throughout most of the coaching process the executive coach will use open-ended rather than closed questions. The simple difference between these two being that closed questions can be answered "Yes" or "No", whereas open ones require longer, more descriptive answers. The aim of open-ended questions is to encourage the client to explore his experience though his descriptive answers. Through description the client will begin to uncover meaning and discover relationships between his thoughts and behaviour which promote his self-awareness. The executive coach will also begin to understand the situation from the perspective of the client. Open-ended questions allow the client to answer in his own terms without being forced to make choices from answer categories presented by the executive coach.

Closed questions also have their place in executive coaching. The use of a closed question can stimulate the client to clear statements and can also test commitment and consent to action, "Are you prepared to do x three times in the next fortnight?"

Experienced executive coaches begin coaching conversations with fairly broad questions. As the conversation progresses the questions will carry an intent to focus in on detail.

Five sets of precise questions, shown in Figure 4 below, can be used to establish meaning and shared understanding. The aim of these questions is to get beneath what is being said to uncover exactly what is meant. The questions tackle three main causes of confusion in executive coaching sessions:

- missing information
- generalization and
- assertion

If these are not clarified the executive coach may make unsubstantiated assumptions.

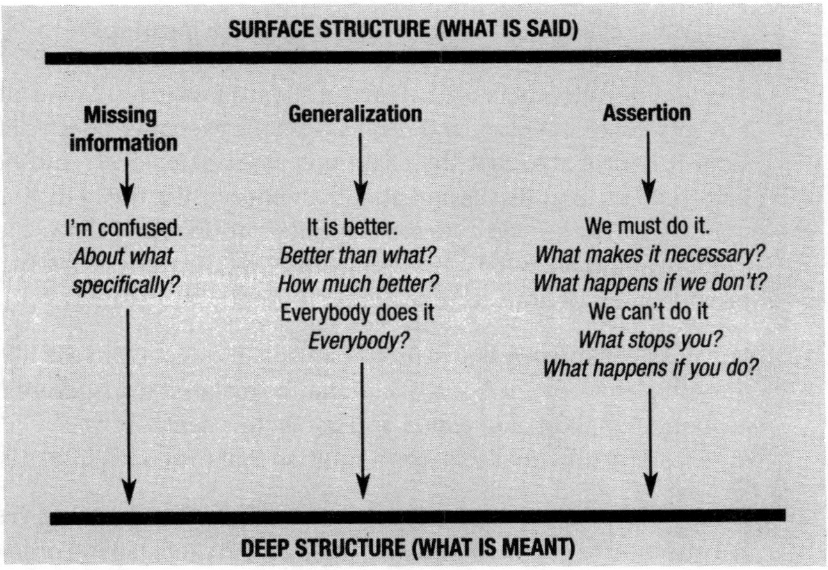

Figure 4: Use of questions to uncover meaning

Getting underneath the surface

The questions allow a 'zooming in' on the critical behaviour that did not lead to the desired outcome and helps to maintain the focus of the client by bringing things to his attention. The process is very much client led as the executive coach follows the client's train of thought. Questioning is intimately linked to the executive coach's listening abilities and an experienced executive coach will also be listening out for what the client is not detailing in his descriptions. This may provide the executive coach with the opportunity to expose the client's blind spots to him using questions such as "I noticed that you have not mentioned ... Is there any particular reason for this?" Increased awareness of these blind spots often leads to action or, as Sir John Whitmore puts it, "The curative properties of awareness are legion!"

Using questions to influence the client is a powerful skill and one that requires the executive coach to think very carefully about the intent behind the question. Almost any question will influence the client's thinking so it is important that your question does not force the choice for the client, limit his options or carry any implied criticism. To explain the difference rather overtly, consider the following two questions:

1. "What caused you to be so oppressive in that meeting?" versus
2. "What caused you to act in that way in the meeting?"

The first question puts a label on the client's behaviour – one which is not very complimentary and results from the executive coach's impression. It is probable that the client will react defensively and become involved in a long discussion about whether or not the behaviour was oppressive. The second question leaves it more open and allows the client to think about what led to the behaviour – an awareness of which may provide more options for behaving differently in the future.

It is possible and can be useful for an executive coach to ask a leading question. However, it is important that he makes it transparent that he is about to make a suggestion and gains the client's permission rather than leading the client towards a solution that the coach thinks is right.

A very useful technique to cultivate is that of probing. A probe in essence is a question or comment designed to keep the client talking or to obtain clarification. It is another coaching technique used to dive deeper into the client's response. Probing can enable the experienced executive coach to go beyond the client's initial answer which can often be an artificial rationalization and/or a socially desired answer. Probes make a client work: they stretch him to articulate what has often not been articulated before and thus may lead to the greatest insights and effective learning.

There are four different types of probes that are valuable in executive coaching:

- silent probe
- conversational probe

- repetitive probe
- last statement probe

Silent probe: Here the executive coach remains silent whilst waiting for the response of the executive. This may be the most challenging probe for the coach. As Sir John Whitmore puts it, "Perhaps the hardest thing a coach has to learn to do is to shut up!" A period of silence is often useful for the client to really explore his emotions and think about a particular topic or situation.

Conversational probe: These are detailed oriented questions like: When...? Who...? When...? This type of probe is valuable to obtain a richer and more detailed picture of some activity or experience.

Repetitive probe: This probe encourages the executive to talk further, keep thinking, digging deeper and exploring more of the area. We have seen and used sequences where we simply asked "What else?" several times with quite astonishing results. In eight out of ten cases this probe led to further insights.

Last statement probe: Here the last words or statements of the executive are used with an increased inflection to gain further clarification.

The use of probes is a powerful and effective technique which forms an integral part of an effective executive coaching toolkit.

SUMMARY: CREATIVE QUESTIONING

Creative questioning is at the heart of effective executive coaching. Asking the right question, at the right time, is central to coaching success.

Questions should always be asked with a specific purpose. The main roles of questions are to:

- compel the client to think, to examine, to look, to feel, to be engaged
- evoke clarity of thinking
- focus attention on critical behaviours/areas
- stimulate answers which are descriptive but not judgemental (to avoid a descent into self-criticism)

- check understanding
- increase the client's self-awareness
- promote the client's responsibility for using his resources and develop solutions
- challenge the client to take action and initiate change
- gain commitment
- obtain high quality feedback which is essential to the forward momentum of the coaching relationship

Effective questions begin with:

- What…?
- When…?
- Who…?
- Where…?

The use of 'why' and 'how' questions should be avoided as these tend to make the client defensive and hinder progress towards his goal.

As the experience of the executive coach grows so does his repertoire of questioning skills, including techniques such as probing. Questions can be used to get beyond superficial answers to uncover the real meaning and increase the client's awareness of his own thinking and actions.

CHAPTER SIX Giving effective feedback

SIX Giving effective feedback

Introduction

Executive coaching is a collaborative process in which the executive coach and client are working together towards the achievement of the client's goal. Listening to the client and asking creative questions are key capabilities but are insufficient on their own to enable the client to reach his goal. Listening and questioning, as we have described them in the preceding chapters, are non-directive techniques. However, in our view, effective executive coaching also requires the executive coach to occasionally apply more directive techniques to adapt to the needs of the client, depending on the specific situation. The range of directive and non-directive techniques are summarized in the Figure below.

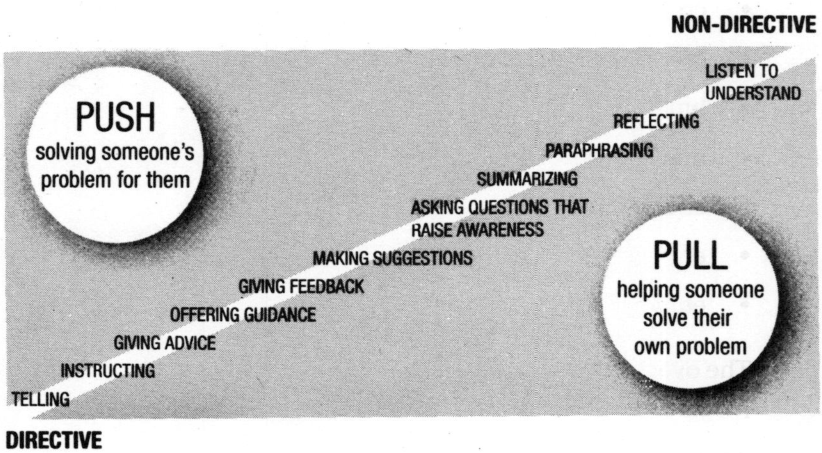

Figure 5: The Coaching Continuum
Source: School of Coaching, 2003

The most effective executive coaching we have experienced is a balance between non-directive techniques like listening to understand, reflecting and the right type of 'telling'. Whereas offering guidance and giving advice depends on the degree of special expertise an executive coach may have, giving effective feedback is a core capability shared by all experienced executive coaches.

Giving feedback is essentially more of a directive technique as it involves the coach making direct statements and observations. In our experience, sooner or later in a coaching process the client will ask for feedback on what you have heard and observed.

What is effective feedback?

In any communication between two people there will be occasions where each is giving and receiving feedback. Simply by making a statement and noting the other person's reaction we are receiving feedback. However, in executive coaching it is the coach's responsibility to provide feedback that is purposeful and with a positive intent.

The aims of effective feedback within the executive coaching context are to:

- create and enhance awareness of the impact the client has on others
- create a greater level of self-understanding
- build skills and/or an idea
- modify behaviour
- encourage productive action
- enhance the client's level of self confidence
- enhance the client's level of well-being

The overall aim is to provide the relevant feedback at the most effective point in the executive coaching process.

At all times in the coaching process it is essential that the feedback focuses on facts and observed behaviour rather than a personal reflection of what the coach thinks of the client.

How to give effective feedback

For some executive coaches using a straightforward 'in-your-face-style' of feedback may work if they have established a good relationship with the client and know his preferred mode of receiving feedback. However, for most executive coaches and in most situations such directness is a gamble and may not be the most effective method for the client.

When speaking with executive coaches we identified that many found giving effective feedback to be one of the most challenging areas, particularly at the start of their executive coaching career. Many were initially quite insecure and most went though a learning curve until they genuinely felt comfortable giving effective feedback.

The origin of this insecurity stems from the nature of the coaching relationship itself. An executive coach is in an unusual and privileged position as the neutral 'sparring partner' to the client. The executive coach is detached from the client's organization and therefore has an opportunity to operate to support the client's agenda. This presents the executive coach with a dilemma.

He recognizes that giving effective feedback is an essential part of the executive coaching process to help the client in his learning and development but if the feedback is not well received then it could damage the coaching relationship,and the relationship with the client's organization. In both cases this could lead to a loss of income. Economic imperatives are only one part of the equation. The executive coach could be equally concerned about the kudos associated with working with a powerful client within the organization and the negative impact of 'upsetting' such a client.

However, more experienced executive coaches recognize that an essential part of the role of an executive coach is to challenge. Executive coaching is not all about being sympathetic and agreeing with the client. To help ensure momentum towards the goal it is important for the executive coach to give feedback which is honest but not judgemental. It may deliver some hard messages but done within the context of a mutually respectful relationship the executive coach can deliver the message in a frank yet graceful manner.

In our practice we have identified seven characteristics of effective feedback in an executive coaching context. Effective feedback is:

- based on a concrete observation rather than an opinion or judgement
- factual rather than evaluative

- provided close to a specific situation rather than after a long time-lapse
- behavioural rather than personal
- specific rather than general
- creative rather than analytical
- supportive rather than defensive

One of the most well-known models of giving feedback is the 'Feedback Sandwich'. This has three stages:

- what went well
- what needs to be improved
- overall positive statement

The model is often used in performance appraisal meetings and has found its way into coaching practices, but has the major disadvantage that the person receiving the feedback may miss what needs to be improved. This is because of the effects of primacy and recency – in other words the client hears what was said first and last, and misses out important information in the middle. An executive coach can assist the client here by asking, "So, what will you do differently next time?"

However, the most effective feedback cycle we identified has five distinct phases which are illustrated in the Figure below.

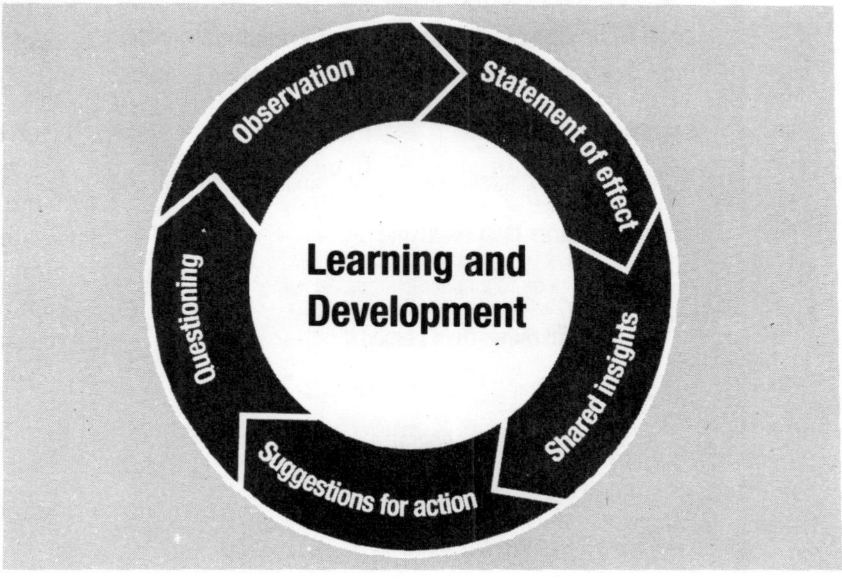

Figure 6: Effective feedback cycle in executive coaching

1. **Observation**: The coach provides a summary of his observations and reflections of what he has seen and heard.
2. **Statement of effect**: The coach explains what impact this has had on him or may have on others using phrases such as "I noticed that you ..." or "It had this effect on me ..."

   This represents a critical first step in the client's learning and development as it raises his awareness of the impact of his behaviour.
3. **Shared insights**: The coach and client share insights about the impact and consequences of the client's actions and behaviour.
4. **Suggestions for action**: The coach provides a concrete and actionable suggestion so that the client has a clear picture about the behavioural alternatives.
5. **Questioning**: The coach asks an open question to move the client forward into taking concrete action.

The feedback cycle proved to be highly effective in the executive coaching context. However, in a real-life context it's not as clear cut as the visualization may suggest.

SUMMARY: EFFECTIVE FEEDBACK

Effective feedback is important because it provides an objective mirror for the client, By reflecting on his behaviour the client can examine the consequences and to make the necessary changes so that goals are achieved.

Effective feedback is:

- based on a concrete observation rather than an opinion or judgement
- factual rather than evaluative
- provided close to a specific situation rather than after a long time-lapse
- behavioural rather than personal
- concrete rather than ephemeral
- specific rather than general
- creative rather than analytical
- supportive rather than defensive

It is also important to think about how to give feedback. We identified and described five phases in an effective feedback cycle:

1. Observation – where the executive coach provides a summary reflecting what he has seen and heard
2. Statement of effect – where, to raise the clients awareness of his behaviour, the executive coach may explain what impact he has noticed either within himself, others or in the client during the discussion
3. Shared insights – where the executive coach and client share insights about the impact or consequences of the clients behaviour
4. Suggestions for action – where the executive coach provides suggestions for alternative courses of action
5. Questioning – where the executive coach asks an open question to move the discussion forward

CHAPTER SEVEN Clear goal setting

SEVEN Clear goal setting

Introduction

Without clear goals, executive coaching relationships can become just a forum for rambling discussions about issues and an opportunity for the client to 'let off steam'. Although there may be benefits to some aspects of this, it is a clear aim of executive coaching for the client to set and achieve goals which are in line with organizational as well as personal objectives. Ironically, many of those who come to coaching are used to clear project management with stated aims, objectives, outputs and outcomes but fail to set these targets or apply the associated skills for themselves and to their own careers.

By setting clear goals clients enhance their ability to self-regulate as it increases motivation towards taking positive action to achieve specific aims, and to enhance persistence and learning. In addition, clear goals allow for self-evaluation of progress which is important if coaching is to contribute to individual learning and development.

It is much easier to articulate what we do not want than to state a positive goal. For example, imagine for a moment that you are sitting in a restaurant; you look at the menu, call the waiter over and say "Well, let's see. I don't want the chicken soup, I don't want the pasta, I don't want the fish, I don't want the steak ..." What happens next is very much dependent on the patience of the waiter. You may get something at the end but unless it is clearly articulated you will not get anything and will end up hungry and frustrated. This is analogous to the client's situation. Without a clear goal for the coaching process he may merely remain dissatisfied and not achieve any forward movement.

What is clear goal setting?

Goal setting in the executive coaching process is essential. The precise formulation of a goal is critical because of the impact it will have on the achievement of the goal. The first and most important feature of a goal is that it is clearly owned by the client. Goals in a business context are more often than not stated with the organization in mind. In our experience it is very important that the goal also has direct personal relevance for the individual. Experienced executive coaches always ensure that the goal is one which is of direct and personal relevance to the client and that it has been initiated by him rather than being driven by an external force such as the organization and/or his partner.

There are several acronyms associated with goal setting which seek to set out the requisite steps in the formulation of a clear goal. From our experience those that have proven to be most useful are those based on the acronyms of SMART, PURE and CLEAR. There is some overlap between the acronyms but we have found it useful to use all three as they do touch upon different areas.

SMART is probably the most well-known acronym of goal setting and this, plus the steps of PURE and CLEAR, will be explained below.

SMART as an acronym for goal setting has been quoted many times. The most common explanation of each of the stages is that a goal needs to be:

- **S**pecific
- **M**easurable
- **A**chievable
- **R**ealistic
- **T**ime bound

The principles of each stage are explained in more detail below.

Specific

The goal needs to be formulated so that it is specific, i.e. clearly defined. This is important because the client is much more likely to accomplish a goal which is clearly defined than one which is more general. This is because in the act of setting a goal the client directs his focus towards the specific aim. We tend to achieve what we focus on rather than what we do not. This is because by making a conscious decision to go towards something we are issuing instructions to our subconscious which will then help us to work towards achieving the goal. For example, have you ever noticed that once you decide on buying a particular car then all you notice everyday are cars that meet your specification. This is because your internal filters which direct the focus of your attention have been briefed with the specification of your desired car.

To set a specific goal, experienced coaches work with the client to elicit answers to the following five questions:

1. **What** – do you want to accomplish? 'What' is also used in this context to ask questions to ascertain the specific reasons behind the desire to achieve the goal and the purpose or benefits of accomplishing the goal.
2. **Who** – is involved? Is it just you or are others involved?
3. **Where** – the context may be important as a behaviour that is appropriate in the work context but which may not be desired at home.
4. **When** – it is important to establish a time frame to establish its immediacy and urgency.
5. **Which** – questions identify which resources and constraints will operate in the achievement of the goal.

Measurable

The executive coach works with the client to establish concrete criteria for measuring progress towards the attainment of the goal. When progress is measured on a continuous basis, the client knows when he is on track and can experience the exhilaration of achievement that will provide a further spur to continued effort. To determine if a goal is measurable we use questions such as:

- How much ...?
- How many?
- How will you know when it is accomplished? What will you see, hear and feel?

Achievable

Goals also need to be formulated so that they can be reached – stretch but not snap. When the client identifies goals that are most important to him you can identify concrete action steps together to realize them. The process of developing the attitude, abilities, skills and capacity to reach the goal follows almost automatically. Suddenly, previously overlooked opportunities to bring the goal closer to achievement come to the fore. There are alternative interpretations of the letter 'a': these are attainable and actionable. All are good and point in the same direction.

Realistic

To be realistic, a goal must represent an objective towards which the client is both willing and able to work. A goal can be both high and realistic. The client is the only person who can decide how high his goal should be. Some experienced executive coaches believe that a high or tough goal is easier to achieve than a low one as it exerts a greater motivational force. They stress that some of the hardest goals a client achieves simply because the client holds the goal in high esteem and regards its achievement as a labour of love. A goal is probably realistic if the client truly believes that it can be accomplished. Alternative interpretations are: reachable and relevant.

Time bound

Clients can achieve a realistic goal they set when they plan their steps wisely and establish a clear time frame that allows them to carry out the critical steps.

Most clients will have an appreciation of SMART goal setting but Sir John Whitmore stresses that a goal also needs to be PURE and CLEAR. These acronyms help the coach to work with the client to clarify the goal so that it becomes more readily achievable.

PURE means:

- **P**ositively stated
- **U**nderstood
- **R**elevant
- **E**thical

Positively stated

Goals need to be stated in the positive. Experienced executive coaches work with the client to formulate a goal which is stated in positive words. For example, if the client says that he wants to "stop wasting time on unnecessary meetings" the executive coach will work with the client to express this in more positive terms, such as, "I want to develop a system which will enable me to get the most out of meetings that I attend."

The reason for putting goals into the positive is that it is impossible for us to focus on things which are stated negatively. If you are told "don't think of a flying pig" you first have to think of the pig flying before you can send instructions to ignore it. Our unconscious minds work entirely on positive suggestions and focus our attention on the attainment of the main subject. So it is important to get the client to focus on what they *do* want rather than what they *do not*. Without this focus they will keep on getting the results that they do not want to achieve.

Understood

For a goal to be fully understood by the client it means that he is aware of, and acknowledges, the impact the attainment of the goal will have on him and those around him. The coach works with the client to ensure that the full implications of attaining the goal have been explored.

Relevant

It is important that the goal has relevance for the client. If it does not, then the level of effort put into achieving the goal may be insufficient. One of the most critical issues is the ownership of the goal. Goals in a business context are more often than not stated with the organization in mind but, as we have stated before, it is critical that they also have direct personal relevance for the individual. Only then will the client be willing to 'do whatever it takes' to achieve the goal.

Ethical

Executive coaches must also seek to ensure that the goals set by their clients are ethical. This is important not only to ensure that the needs of the organization and client are met but also to maintain professional practice.

To provide a further check on the definition of the goal, **CLEAR** is also used. The acronym CLEAR represents:

- **C**hallenging
- **L**egal
- **E**nvironmentally sound
- **A**ppropriate
- **R**ecorded

Challenging

A goal needs to challenge the client. Without a challenge the client is unlikely to move forwards as achieving the goal may not move him beyond his current state. However, it is important to maintain a careful balance between stretch and snap. If the goal is at either extreme then the client is unlikely to put in sufficient effort to achieve the goal and become disillusioned with the whole coaching process.

Legal

All goals must be within the context of the legal framework of the organization and the country.

Environmentally sound

The coach works through the goal with the client to ensure that it is appropriate in the client's overall life context.

Appropriate

The goal should fit the abilities and personality of the client. It is most crucial that the goal is defined by the client.

Recorded

The coach should also ensure that the goal is written down so that there is a permanent record of it and to ensure commitment.

Although there are some overlaps between the different acronyms they touch on different aspects. Together they provide easy to recall guidance within a coaching context. This allows executive coaches to check the goal in the coaching session and ensure that the client really examines the goal and its impact before embarking on a course of action towards achieving it.

The graph below shows the effect of increasing difficulty on the attainment of a goal. If the goal is too difficult to achieve then any effort will just 'fizzle out'. Conversely, if it is not stretching then the effort that the client puts into its achievement is disproportionately less.

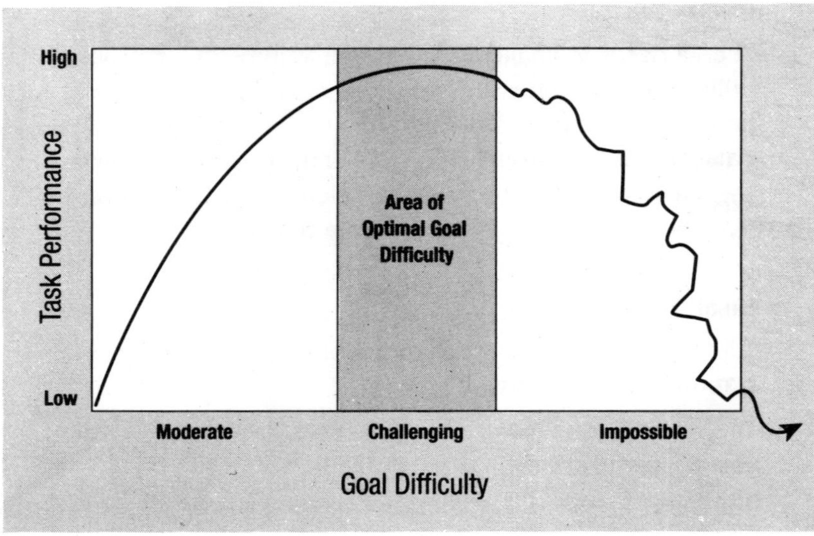

Figure 7: Effect of goal difficulty on performance
Source: Robbins B.P. and Langton N. (2003) Organizational Behavior, Pearson Education

The most effective solution in the executive coaching context is to develop goals that are realistic yet challenging in order to be motivating.

Six distinct qualities of a well-composed goal

From our experience of using the processes of goal-setting we identified the following six distinct qualities of a well-composed goal:

1. The goal really matters to the executive

The goal needs to be relevant and meaningful for the executive on a deeply personal level – it really needs to matter. If the goal is 'just' socially desired or of relevance to the organization, it is not sufficient to create the force and motivation that will lead to the achievement of the goal.

2. The goal is challenging and broken down into achievable chunks

We recognized that there needs to be a fine balance between a goal that is attainable and one that is challenging enough to act as a magnet towards its achievement. As the challenging goal may be out of immediate reach we recognized that it is important that the goal is broken down into achievable chunks. This provides small successes along the way to the achievement of the end goal and helps both client and executive coach to recognize and celebrate progress.

3. The goal is realistic within the context of the executive's life

Executive coaching goals tend to be bound within the client's organizational context. We recognized that clients have a far higher chance of achieving goals if they are ecological, that is have a fit to the overall life of the client.

4. The goal is stated in a positive and proactive language

This forces the executive to think about the presence of something desirable or of a specific behaviour. If you want to get anywhere you actually have to say where you do want to go. It helps both the executive and his executive coach to determine if something has been achieved.

5. The goal is concrete, specific and behavioural

It is difficult to measure progress towards a goal unless it is concrete. For example, it is much easier to assess progress towards, "jogging five miles twice a week" than "by September I will be fitter than I am now".

6. The client views the goal as involving personal 'action'

This compels the executive to take personal responsibility for achieving the goal.

In our opinion goal setting is likely to increase in importance within the executive coaching context. This is because within organizations there are increasing pressures to demonstrate a positive return on investment from training and development interventions such as executive coaching. (See also chapter 18.)

SUMMARY: GOAL SETTING

Goal setting is important because it sets direction and provides a clear aim for the coaching sessions. In addition, by setting and achieving goals the executive coach and the client can demonstrate the return on investment to the organization.

Three acronyms are used as mnemonics to guide executive coaches and clients through the process of goal setting. These are:

- SMART: Specific, Measurable, Achievable, Realistic and Time bound
- PURE: Positively stated, Understood, Relevant and Ethical
- CLEAR: Challenging, Legal, Environmentally sound, Appropriate and Recorded

A well composed goal has six distinct qualities:

- the goal really matters to the executive
- the goal is challenging and broken down into achievable chunks
- the goal is realistic within the context of the executive's life
- the goal is stated in a positive and proactive language
- the goal is concrete, specific and behavioural
- the client views the goal as involving personal 'action'.

CHAPTER EIGHT Intuition

EIGHT Intuition

Introduction

In many cases when we were talking to experienced executive coaches after a session, we found that they could not provide an explanation for why they had asked a specific question at a particular point. Typically they made a statement such as, "it just seemed the right thing to do at the time." Some of the characteristics of excellent executive coaching cannot be explained by merely pointing to the expertise and experience of the coach with core capabilities such as listening or questioning. There is another component that needs to be considered, and that is intuition. We found many examples of intuition at work in executive coaching assignments.

Knowing which question to ask, which piece of feedback to select and when to probe deeper might be attributed to experience and recognition of familiar patterns. However, sometimes a client will refer to the coach's question as 'inspired' or to a particular discussion as, "That was the moment which seemed to unlock the situation for me." Neither executive coach nor client can consciously explain exactly what happened but the client knows that that was a pivotal point or question. Such inspiration on behalf of the executive coach may be attributed to intuition.

What is intuition?

Intuition has often been placed second to the scientific rigour of analysis using conscious thought when deciding which interpretation of a situation or prediction of future events to rely upon. The status of intuition as a lower order ability may in part be due to the difficulty in defining it, and it may also be that many explanations of intuition are expressed with emotional phrases such as 'gut feeling' to describe the phenomenon. Using phrases such as this suggest that there is no scientific basis for intuition or that it is irrational. Such categorization throws doubt on its validity or trustworthiness and hence intuition is often disregarded.

However, during recent years there has been a resurgence of interest in intuition from a range of disciplines as diverse as engineering to psychology, business and management. The Myers Briggs and other psychological instruments recognize the presence of intuition in management decision-making. Charles Handy talks of 'intuitive intelligence' and describes it as the ability to see and sense what is not immediately obvious. Handy contrasts this with analytical intelligence which is the ability to reason and conceptualize. To illustrate this he refers to discussions with his wife where she has said "You have won the argument but I am right" and acknowledges that she quite often is.

The reasons for this renewed interest may be due to an awareness that the challenges facing a rapidly changing society are too complex to be resolved by rational thoughts alone and that intelligence is composed of more than a rational dimension. Rational thought is analytical, linear and tends to favour deductive reasoning whereas intuition is more 'big picture', holistic and favours inductive reasoning.

Intuition is, therefore, the term applied to describe the ways in which we gain access to and use the full spectrum of the brain's potential unencumbered by the constraints of logical thinking. Intuition combines experience and information from a wide range of sources: emotional, physical and instinctive, some which seem to be outside normal ranges of conscious perception. It enables us to rapidly integrate and address data from past experience, present observation and future anticipation to make sense of a complex situation at a subconscious level. As coaching skills develop, this is an ability which grows and provides one of the hallmarks of excellence in executive coaching and the 'flashes of inspiration' experienced by coaches and their clients.

It is probable that much intuition depends on visual processing. This is indicated by the speed at which information is processed and because much of the language of imagination, dreams and fantasy is visual, indicating its fundamental importance as a primary mode of thinking.

Researchers investigating the process of intuition have examined the capacity of those who demonstrate high levels of intuition such as the chess 'Grand Masters' who can play up to 50 opponents simultaneously. When asked how this was possible, the Grand Masters put it down to their professional skill and intuition. What is happening is that the Grand Masters are playing so frequently that they develop the ability to recognize and process information in 'patterns' or 'blocks' that form the basis for intuitive decisions. The chess masters' mental structure not only organizes the pieces but also suggests which lines of play should be explored by 'seeing' what will happen as a consequence of the moves they decide to make. Intuitive decisions occur much more rapidly than those which require cognitive effort and hence the experienced player wastes far less time in exploring unproductive lines of play than the novice. The process is inductive, drawing on past experience and knowledge to interpret present, and predict future actions.

Within an executive coaching context, the highly experienced executive coach is in a similar position to the chess masters described above. It appears as if experienced executive coaches are able, through intuition, to access vast stores of experience, knowledge and wisdom in a way that sometimes defies logic.

Executive coaches make use of intuition in a number of different situations within the course of a coaching assignment:

- The executive coach allows an intuitive thought to direct the course of questioning to focus and/or zoom in on specific issues, although guards against drawing conclusions too fast. In this context Meryl Martin, a recognized US intuition expert, referred to the old Zen saying, "First thought, best thought."
- The executive coach uses intuition to check for congruency. In other words, the coach compares what is being said with some other communication, such as what the client is doing, how they are sitting etc, to ensure that the words and actions are matching and thus confirming the client's commitment to what they are saying.
- The executive coach is interested in the 'space between the words' and allows himself to explore what is not said.
- The executive coach accepts that intuition may work on little or no consciously available information and allows himself to follow a path even if he does not know where it will lead.
- The executive coach sometimes relinquishes the drive towards a specific outcome for every part of the coaching process by allowing his intuition to direct the flow of the process. In this way, as one executive coach described it "things just happen" and the coach is less likely to attempt to direct the client towards a specific outcome.

The use of intuition within an executive coaching relationship can enrich the process and lead to breakthroughs. However, it is important that the coach should guard against preconceptions and premature closure, i.e. leaping to conclusions. The executive coach needs to listen to and acknowledge intuition, use it, maybe write down a thought and come back to it at a later stage in the context of wider information.

How to hone intuition

If intuition is a basic human capability then it is something which can be further developed and honed once the process and the steps of the process are understood.

One of the issues in understanding and studying intuition is that it is a silent and unconscious process. It is not possible to ask an intuitive person, "What are you doing?" because they are likely to be unaware of exact steps. Our understanding comes from observing the application of intuition and the resulting action.

When we talked to experienced executive coaches we recognized that they had made a conscious effort to rediscover their intuitive abilities. In everyday life many things contribute to the suppression of intuition and we are encouraged to think and act rationally. By taking time out to reflect and contemplate, the coaches were allowing themselves to 'tune in' to their intuition. This ability to 'tune in' is rather like tuning in to a distant radio station – the signals are always there, they just are not received unless the dial is set to that particular channel. To develop the necessary time and space to become reacquainted with intuition, the coaches used a variety of tactics ranging from gardening and long walks with their dog, to more deliberate relaxation techniques such as yoga and meditation.

By training ourselves to be aware of how our intuition works we develop new connections in our brains that make us more accepting of intuition and potentially more creative with it.

Of course, intuition is only one of the core capabilities. We see it as an important capability, but not the most important capability. The use of intuition has to be to complement the application of a systematic approach, the development of excellence with the more cognitive capabilities, and a high and positive regard for the client acquired through sound and rigorous executive coach training and practice and experience. Only by combining all capabilities, sources and information can coaches operate at their most effective level.

SUMMARY: INTUITION

Intuition is where the executive coach uses the full spectrum of his experience and knowledge to help interpret a particular event or situation described by the client that goes beyond an assessment of the situation that could be achieved by purely analytical thinking. Intuition is non-linear and very powerful though hard to define. It's something we all know when we feel it.

The use of intuition complements the other core capabilities by adding an additional dimension to the understanding of a client's situation and the steps he needs to take to achieve his goal.

Intuition can be enhanced by taking time out for reflection and through practical experience of trusting and following hunches. The use of intuition can enrich the process and lead to significant breakthroughs.

However, insights gained through intuition need to be tested with the client to avoid:

a) the development of solutions arrived at by 'jumping to conclusions' and

b) the premature close down of discussions without fully exploring an issue

CHAPTER NINE Presence

NINE Presence

Introduction

Presence is a very elusive and enigmatic capability. It is difficult to define, yet most people would clearly recognize it when they see and feel it. What is more, nearly everyone would agree that it is one of the most admired qualities any individual can possess.

Presence could be likened to charisma but not everyone with presence would fit the typical description of a charismatic person – some quiet, unassuming individuals exhibit presence in abundance. Detecting presence in someone else is relatively easy. You sense that the individual is at peace and at home with himself. You feel drawn towards them and they exhibit an ability to engage, inspire, enliven, delight and motivate others. They inspire trust, generate a 'feel-good factor' and you seek out their company. Presence is also something which you recognize in another in a very short space of time. If you think back to schooldays you knew very quickly if a new teacher had presence or not (probably when they first entered the room) and reacted to them accordingly!

What is presence?

But what exactly is 'presence'? One definition is that it is 'a person's force of personality'. This force is meant in a positive sense and describes the personal energy emanating from someone rather than an oppressive, domineering force. However, it is insufficient to just 'be yourself' as an executive coach. To be successful an executive coach also needs to ensure that he works on self-presentation to allow all the positive elements to shine through.

Within the coaching context the possession of presence has implications for the initial selection of an executive coach and for their credibility. Coaching clients described to us that when they were choosing their executive coach only part of the decision was based on credentials, background and references, the other part was basically 'gut feel'. As a German manager of a large telecommunications company described, "It was somehow a reaction to her presence ... that just resonated with me."

In contrast those executive coaches that possessed all the basic core capabilities, methods, tools and techniques but were lacking in presence were considered less suitable. So, presence is important as a capability and may even determine the extent of your success as an executive coach – the question remains as to whether it is just something that you 'just have' or whether it can be developed.

How to develop presence

We believe that presence, like leadership, is a quality which can be developed. We all have a personal presence which others can detect. It is a feature of the personal energy that we, and all living things, possess. Every living thing has an energy field.

What do we mean by 'personal energy'? We are all, of course, aware of our own personal energy levels. We know when we feel energetic and when we feel drained. These physical manifestations of our energy levels affect our coaching relationships and it is important to be in peak state when coaching executives. However, in this context we are discussing the energy which others can detect emanating from you. In coaching and other interpersonal interactions it is possible to develop and influence the impact that this has on others. On a practical level the coach can demonstrate this by expressing positive emotions and by demonstrating an optimistic outlook when talking to the client. For example, when working with a newly appointed leader the executive coach may say something such as, "Yes, we can work together on the steps that will be necessary to make you a more effective leader." This boosts both the client's self-confidence and his confidence in the executive coach and the process.

In our own practice and from observing others it is obvious that some executive coaches are more energetic than others. What is less obvious is how one energetic coach is perceived as inspiring and others are described by their clients as "hyperactive and distracting". While both groups of executive coaches have an abundance of energy, the person with 'presence' appears to know how to channel it effectively. It appears to be the management, focus and intelligent transmission of personal energy that makes the difference between an executive coach with presence and one who is viewed as distracting. So, it is not about how *much* energy you radiate, it is about *how* you use it.

In learning to use energy positively, it is important to remember that we can control where the energy flows and from where it is sourced. Energy flows where you focus your attention. There is a world of difference between the energy directed towards an individual you are seeking to help achieve his goals, and one in whom you have a romantic interest. It is therefore important to be aware of this and make sure that you are always operating from a position of personal and professional integrity.

So, one of the keys to developing presence in executive coaching is the management and focus of personal energy levels. The process begins in the mind and the focus of the mind directs the way in which we act. In our own practice we have found that the skill lies in focusing and deploying personal energy within a coaching session where the need for impact is the greatest. It also involves the two-way flow of communication – being an attentive and active listener and picking up on the executive's feelings, concerns and anxieties.

Acting is another profession which requires the development of presence. To provide a further explanation of the process, consider a great acting performance you have experienced. A great performance is marked out by the apparent ease with which the actor performs his part and by the way that he is able to become the character he portrays. This is only possible if the actor has thought himself into the part and entered into the character so that everything he does and says is congruent with the character. This applies equally to executive coaches. There must be a correlation between what is communicated verbally and non-verbally. If there is a mismatch between the verbal and non-verbal components, it appears to be almost impossible for the executive coach to maintain rapport and trust, which are themselves important components of presence.

We noticed that experienced executive coaches with presence are highly skilled masters of rapport. They use many non-verbal clues of openness – open body posture, keep their hands apart and maintain good eye contact with the client. When speaking they make use of vocal variety and use animated facial expressions to signify interest and generate enthusiasm. They also lean in slightly towards the client to show attention and to encourage the client to keep talking.

While it is important to show synchronicity with the client, we want to inject a word of caution – great rapport, and hence presence, cannot be faked. In research at Oregon State University, Professor Bernieri stressed that people will notice, albeit unconsciously, if their movements are mimicked intentionally. One of his graduate students had conducted research where they set up interview situations. Half of the group received instructions to deliberately mimic the interviewer; the other half received no instructions. The interviewers had no knowledge of the instructions given to the group yet intuitively liked those participants who mimicked them naturally. They remained neutral, however, to those who had mimicked them intentionally. The implication for executive coaches is that it is important to practise the behaviours and skills which make up presence so that they become second nature. Great coaches show self-consistency with their behaviours over time.

The client is more likely to open up and fully explore an issue if the coach is also open and straight in every verbal and non-verbal communication. One very experienced executive coach said to us that, "It is crucial to put any of your own fears aside, to talk openly of things that maybe social convention dictates are not appropriate in a work context. This demonstrates integrity to the client and those coaches that shy away from it may not gain the respect and success they are seeking."

Genuine presence appears to play a major role in the success of an executive coach. Whilst it can be argued if, and to what extent, it actually can be learned, one thing is certain, it cannot be just an act.

SUMMARY: PRESENCE

Presence can be defined as being a person's force of personality or personal energy level. It is the factor that helps people get noticed in a crowded room. Clients will often select an executive coach to work with on their presence or energy levels and not just because of their credentials, training and qualifications. Presence is an important factor both in the initial selection of an executive coach and in the development of the ongoing coaching relationship.

Presence, like leadership skills, can be to a certain extent learnt and enhanced through positive self-presentation and the development of skills, knowledge and experience.

It takes the entire suite of the seven core capabilities to create an executive coaching dialogue that informs, enriches and engages clients enough to make them widen their behavioural repertoire and achieve the desired results.

The challenge for executive coaches is to focus on their own qualities and develop their own unique potential on their own terms and in their own time so that they are operating from a position of integrity and authenticity. There is an old saying in the helping professions, "You can only take the client as far as you are in your own development." In this, coaching is no different and coaches must continuously look to their own personal and professional development to ensure that they are best placed to help their clients.

PART TWO OVERALL SUMMARY: THE SEVEN CORE CAPABILITIES OF EXECUTIVE COACHING

This part has described in-depth the seven core capabilities of executive coaching. These are:

- rapport building
- deep listening
- creative questioning
- clear goal setting
- giving effective feedback
- intuition
- presence

The successful experienced executive coach makes use of a personal blend of all seven of these skills and abilities. Depending on the situation and the context of the coaching issue, an effective executive coach will lay greater emphasis on one or two of the core capabilities at any particular time. However, to be fully effective the executive coach will need to be professionally fluent across all capabilities. This part has explained each capability in depth and made suggestions on how to develop each capability.

PART THREE

The Achieve Coaching Model® – the systematic approach to effective executive coaching

Introduction

At the heart of our international executive coaching practice is the Achieve Coaching Model®. The model is based on insights gained in our international best practice study in executive coaching and was further tested and refined through our own international executive coaching practice. We wanted to develop a coaching model which reflected the best practice we experienced and one that was really practical and relevant for use in executive coaching programmes. We also wanted a model that would help build effective, systematic and sustainable coaching relationships.

One of the key findings of our best practice study is that experienced coaches who achieve tangible and sustainable results in their coaching, consciously or unconsciously, use a seven step approach.

In this part we provide detailed descriptions of each step of the Achieve Coaching Model®. Each step of the model is described in detail and enriched with 'real life' know-how, examples and quotes under the following headings:

- **General description**.
- **Objectives**. Here we detail the specific objectives of the step and the contribution to the overall outcome of the coaching programme.
- **Observations of the key effective behaviours of experienced executive coaches**. Here we describe the key behaviours of experienced executive coaches, i.e. experienced coaches who consistently achieve tangible and sustainable outcomes in their executive coaching assignments.
- **Top tips**. Here we highlight top tips from experienced executive coaches to enhance executive coaching practice internationally.
- **The client perspective**. Here we provide descriptions and insights from our interviews and feedback sessions with clients.
- **Case study**. Here we provide a case example from our own international executive coaching practice to highlight the use of the model in a 'real life' setting.

As with any model it is important to exercise caution. It may appear from the graphical representation (see Figure 9) that the coaching process is one which neatly follows a linear path. In practice, this is not the case.

Executive coaching is more of an iterative process where the coach and client are working backwards and forwards through the process. Executive coaches should also be wary of following the model mechanistically moving from one step to another. It is imperative, however, to ensure that all stages are covered in an executive coaching programme in order to achieve a measurable and sustainable outcome.

In our own coaching practice we work with the model and have tested it in various countries, industries, situations and at different hierarchical levels within an organization. The feedback we have received from organizations and individual clients suggests that the use of the systematic processes of the model achieves the client's desired results.

The GROW Model

The GROW Model was used as the starting point for the development of the Achieve Coaching Model®. The GROW Model, developed by Graham Alexander and racing champion Sir John Whitmore, is the best-known coaching model in the UK and the one that is most widely used in coaching assignments in industry.

A recent study conducted by the Work Foundation and the School of Coaching[3] revealed that 34% of participating respondents drawn from a panel of FTSE 100 organizations and other organizations stated that they used the GROW Model. About one third cited they used a variety of models and the remaining third did not know what models or processes were used in their coaching activities.

What does the acronym GROW actually stand for? GROW stands for:

- **G**oal
- **R**eality
- **O**pportunity
- **W**ill/wrap up/what next?

Footnote: 3 Scoular, A. (2002), What is the Basis of UK Coaching?, Paper Series School of Coaching.

GOAL	REALITY
• Agree on topic for discussion • Agree on specific outcomes • Set long-term aims if appropriate	• Invite self-assessment • Offer specific examples of feedback • Avoid or check assumptions • Discard irrelevant history
OPPORTUNITY • Cover the full range of options • Invite suggestions from the client • Offer suggestions carefully • Ensure choices are made	**WILL/WRAP UP/WHAT NEXT?** • Prepare a plan • Identify possible obstacles • Make steps specific and define timing • Agree support

Figure 8: The GROW Model

The GROW Model provides a framework of four main stages for a coaching session. During the first stage of a session, coach and client develop agreement on specific outcomes and objectives – the goal for the coaching programme.

During the second stage, the coach works with the client to explore the reality of their current situation. In this stage the coach uses a range of techniques including inviting self-assessment, asking specific and challenging questions and offering feedback.

In the third stage, the coach works with the client to generate and choose between options for action that will move the client closer to his goal.

In the final stage, the client commits to action. The coach works with the client to define an action plan and identifies potential obstacles and how to overcome them.

The first three stages are all designed to increase the client's awareness of himself, his situation and his possibilities for action. The final stage is all about evoking the client's responsibility to take action.

The popularity and appeal of the model is that it provides a systematic, memorable framework that describes a rather complex process like executive coaching. At the same time it is practical.

The Achieve Coaching Model®

So what is the Achieve Coaching Model®? An early version emerged from our international best practice study of executive coaching. We found that experienced executive coaches go beyond the confines of the GROW Model to achieve measurable and sustainable results with their clients. Over time we have refined the model on the basis of our experience in international coaching assignments.

The Achieve Coaching Model® details a systematic coaching process which makes the whole executive coaching process transparent for:

- organizations who wish to implement a systematic process to achieve measurable and sustainable outcomes, and a greater ROI from their spend on executive coaching
- executive coaches who wish to enhance their own coaching practice
- executives thinking about embarking on a coaching programme and who want to know what to expect

The seven stages of the Achieve Coaching Model® are:

- Assess the current situation
- Creative brainstorming of alternatives
- Hone goals
- Initiate options
- Evaluate options
- Valid action programme design
- Encourage momentum

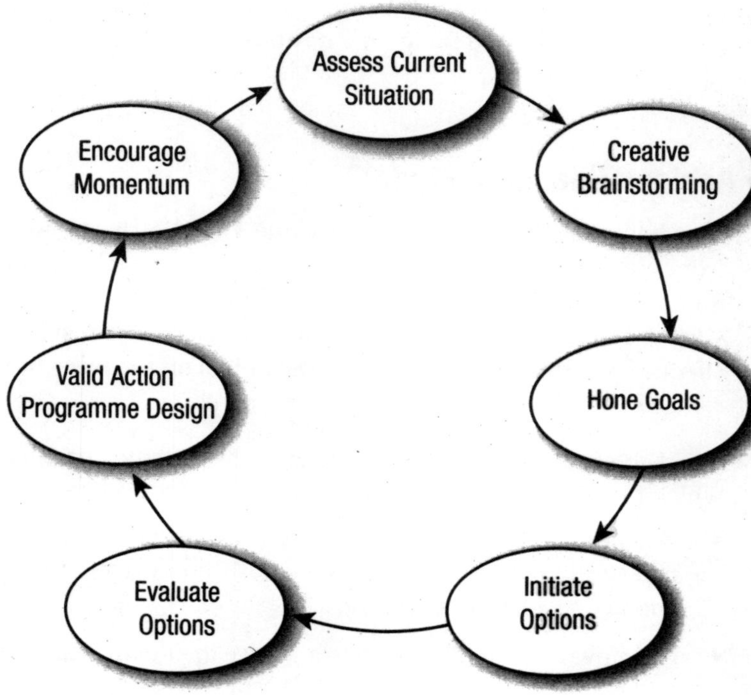

Figure 9: The Achieve Coaching Model®

In the rest of this part we focus on describing the individual stages of the Achieve Coaching Model®.

CHAPTER TEN Step 1: Assessing the current situation

TEN Step 1: Assessing the current situation

General description

Here the executive is encouraged to take time for deep reflection about his current situation. This enhances the executive's self-awareness and helps him identify areas to work on with the executive coach.

The first working coaching session is critical for developing a climate of trust, openness and honesty which is essential for an effective coaching relationship.

By describing the current situation the executive is providing the executive coach with a useful context to help prepare for the sessions ahead. However, the most important benefit of this stage is that the client has an opportunity to reflect and enhance his understanding of what has occurred. In addition, the client has the time and space to consider which specific actions they took contributed to the situation and how they may have stimulated others' responses.

The understanding of the importance of this stage of the coaching process can be enhanced by reference to the Johari Window. The Johari Window model was developed by American psychologists Joseph Luft and Harry Ingham in the 1950s, when they were researching group dynamics. The name was devised from a combination of their first names. The model helps to identify the areas a client needs to explore to enhance his self-awareness.

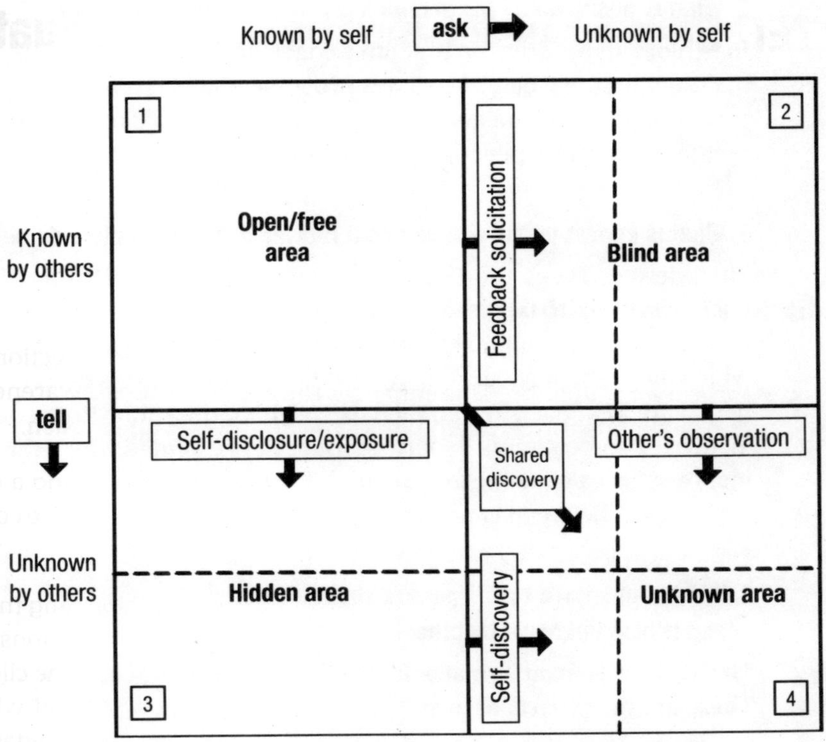

Figure 10: The Johari Window model

The Johari Window represents information – feelings, experience, views, attitudes, skills, intentions and motivation amongst other emotions – within or about a person – in relation to their group, from four different views, which are described below. In assessing the current situation the executive coach and the client explore each of the four areas drawing on information from all available sources.

The four areas are:

1. What is known by the person about himself and is also known by others

Of all the areas this is the easiest to access in an executive coaching conversation. With the right questions and a good level of rapport the client will talk freely and openly about the issues that are known to him and others.

2. What is unknown by the person about himself but which others know

In exploring this area the executive coach and client will use the results of carefully constructed feedback processes such as 360° feedback and psychometric instruments that involve other stakeholders such as subordinates, superiors, peers and clients.

3. What is known by the person about himself but which others do not know

This view requires the coach to develop rapport with the client to encourage him to talk freely and openly. The executive coach needs to exercise deep listening skills to access both what is said and also that which the client may be holding back. Once the coach has detected areas which are held back he can then use probing questions to uncover the 'held back' information. In our experience the extent to which this information is revealed to the executive coach depends upon the level of trust and respect between coach and client.

4. What is unknown by the person about himself and is also unknown by others

This view will become smaller in an effective executive coaching process. There are three parts to this:

1. the element of self discovery
2. others' observations and
3. shared discovery

At the beginning of a coaching assignment the executive coach will work with the client to guide him through the process of increasing self-awareness using a variety of techniques to uncover the information contained within each of the four quadrants.

An increased level of self-awareness will help the client to discover more of his authentic self and provide a direction that is more in line with who he genuinely is. By 'authentic' we mean behaviour that is true to the client's real values and beliefs rather than acting in a way that is socially desirable. Social desirability is the tendency to act in a way which may not truly reflect the client's beliefs and values but which may be desirable from a social standpoint.

We observe many executives who behave in a way that they believe is socially desirable and fail to reflect on whether or not this is true for them or genuinely serves their long-term interests. We work on the premise that only those who behave from an authentic position can be truly successful in the long term.

Sustainable success comes from behaviour that is consistent with personal values and beliefs. If the executive does not recognize this and consistently operates according to an agenda set by others, or is driven by the need to adopt socially desirable positions, then he is likely to experience frustrations, lack of satisfaction and, potentially, 'burn out'.

The catalyst for starting an executive coaching programme will vary but is generally associated with one of the following spurs:

- a clearly identified development need
- a desire to develop further as a person
- a desire to progress further and faster professionally
- dissatisfaction with some aspect of the current work/life situation
- a concern about the individual's preparation for the future

In some instances the client has a sense of the broad direction for the coaching programme but no clarity about which specifics to focus on. In fact most clients can describe what they do not want in great detail but are less articulate about what they actually do want.

Thus, the specific goal is rarely clear at the beginning of an executive coaching programme. Merely asking the client, "What's the goal for this coaching programme?" may result either in silence or seizing upon the first thing that comes to mind which may not tackle root causes or resolve the situation at all.

It is most important to understand the world as viewed by the executive – that is to understand on what principles he operates and how life seems to him. Experienced executive coaches take the time to really understand the situation from the client's perspective, rather than jumping to pre-emptive conclusions and early solution generation. This allows the coach to understand the other person better and to lay a firm foundation of trust between the two parties from which can grow an effective coaching relationship.

It is useful for the executive coach to develop an understanding of the current situation from a variety of perspectives such as:

- the organization
- superiors

- peers
- the team
- customers/clients

Experienced executive coaches include a variety of perspectives and areas of a client's life in their discussions at the first stage of the assessment. As one of the coaches we interviewed in Germany explained, "... you cannot separate the different areas of an executive's life or for that matter anyone's life – they are an interlinked system."

The objectives

The objectives of this stage are:

- laying the foundations of trust for an effective coaching relationship
- understanding the issues, situation and the context of the client
- understanding the world from the point of view of the client
- understanding and identifying development areas
- identifying the most critical development issues

Starting points for an executive coaching assignment

The starting point for an executive coaching assignment can vary greatly. It can be the result of:

- a management audit
- a 360° feedback process
- psychometric instruments
- positive reviews that identified the executive as a 'high potential' or 'future leader'
- identified development needs

Management audit

The starting point for an executive coaching process can be a management audit. Management audits tend to be conducted by an external HR consultancy or executive search firm. In these audits a variety of tests/instruments are used in combination with interviews by a range of stakeholders. These can be superiors, peers, direct reports, customers/clients and subordinates down the reporting line. At the end of this process a report is produced and fed back to the organization as well as the executive. The reports usually highlight the characteristics of the executive, his strengths and development needs. One of the natural next steps is a tailored executive coaching programme.

360° feedback process

The starting point can also be a 360° feedback process. There are now many web-based systems where a large number of people in an organization can be included. In addition, there are more individualized approaches for the top management where personal 360° interviews are still conducted.

The process generates a report that displays areas of strength as well as developmental issues. Some processes also present visual interpretations of the results and comments about the relative performance of the client in relation to other internal and external executives. The report provides the foundation for a structured in-depth feedback discussion during which a personal development plan is created and action steps clearly identified.

Psychometric instruments

The starting point can also be any psychometric instrument. These are used to measure people's skills, abilities, interests or other aspects of behaviour in job-related situations. The assumption of psychometric instruments is that people's performances can be measured on a standard task and compared to other people taking the test, no matter where or when the test is taken. The instruments fall into three broad categories:

- ability
- interest
- personality

A table of commonly used instruments is included in Appendix 2 at the end of the book. Some of the instruments require professional training before they can be administered, whereas others can be administered without training. Executive coaches may have the required formal training or decide to rely on others to conduct the tests. In addition, the client may already have received the results as part of an assessment exercise.

Positive reviews

The starting point can also be following positive reviews that highlight great performance at the executive's current level that classify him as belonging to the category of 'high potentials' or 'future leaders'. We have seen innovative future leader programmes in organizations that provide a development budget for those belonging to this group which provides access to a range of options including in-house training programmes, programmes with external training partners and universities, and executive coaching.

Coaching may also be initiated as the result of a direct request from the executive or his line manager to address assistance in specific situations and development needs.

The information from any of the sources above may be used to inform this first stage of the executive coaching process. One thing we have noted is that some executive coaches do not want to come to the assignment with any preconceptions and make the conscious decision not to review any material prior to the first meeting with the executive. To avoid the formation of preconceptions they will first meet the executive before incorporating other information from any other sources. These executive coaches make informed use of the results of assessments and other information but do not rely solely on any one source.

Key behaviours of experienced executive coaches

• Understands how to create a real sense of relatedness and comfort to foster a climate of openness and trust for the relationship
• Listens deeply so that the client is fully engaged and feels genuinely understood and valued
• Takes time to really understand the situation from the client's perspective
• Observes and takes notice of all verbal and non-verbal communication
• Has a genuine interest and visible enthusiasm for the life stories of executives
• Makes informed use of assessment instruments but does not rely solely on them to gain an understanding of the client's situation

Table 1: Key behaviours of experienced executive coaches in assessing the current situation

Top tips

- **Allow for and be able to endure 'silence'**. Silence can feel embarrassing or threatening. But silence creates a space where an issue can really sink in and the emotional relevance becomes heightened. You should avoid the temptation to break into this space by feeling forced to 'speed the process up' or doing something 'so that the client realizes that you are worth your fees'.
- **Allow a process of co-discovery**. Both the executive coach and the executive are experts in various ways and need to take their time to really understand the underlying issues. Far too often, in their desire to be helpful, executive coaches jump from preliminary problem identification to quick solutions. Only when the underlying problem is clear can sustainable solutions develop that address the causes rather than the symptoms.

- **Explore the context**. It is extremely helpful to explore whether a specific behaviour or event is common or only occurs in a particular context. This will indicate whether the changes that are required are major, affecting many areas of a client's life, or just one specific area. If there are commonalities, explore the similarities across these different situations. If there are differences, explore the factors/issues that make the situations different.
- **Show genuine empathy**. At the beginning of a coaching relationship or a coaching session it is essential for the coach to demonstrate empathy and acknowledge the client and their current experience, i.e. "Sounds like a terrible experience for you..." or "Sounds like a tough lesson for someone who is new in this post ..."
- **'Triangulate' to discover the executive's real needs**. The term triangulation refers to the process of cross-referencing at least three different sources for the same story. The process ensures that multiple points of view are acknowledged and hence increases the chances of identifying the critical themes and patterns. In the context of executive coaching it means not relying on a single source such as the results of a management audit. To gain a rounded picture, draw information from other sources as well – an interview with a superior or subordinate, observation from a team meeting and the coaching conversation itself.

From the client's perspective

Coaching clients have told us that "it feels good to talk about the stuff that is more often than not simply held back." Some found the experience of assessing the current situation energizing, others challenging. Those that described it as challenging said it was best described as "... using an untrained muscle."

In other cases clients describe their initial scepticism about the effectiveness of a stage where all they seemed to be doing was talking in a roundabout or unfocused manner. "At first I thought what a waste of space. Let's cut to the chase and tell me what I need to do to get out of this mess. As we talked more and more I noticed that I started to really understand the whole situation. I noticed that I was thinking differently about my situation. As we progressed through the programme I became aware that I started to come up with ideas and solutions I hadn't thought of before."

Clients also fed back that this is a stage where in-depth reflection takes place and insights begin to emerge. One client told us, "I'm not sure when, if ever before, I just sat for two hours and talked about my current job and all the hassle that comes with the position. For such a long time I've put on a brave face. I didn't talk about work at home – the marriage was nearly on the rocks as it was and I was a virtual stranger to the kids. Strangely, initially I felt tired after the sessions but on the upside there were strong feelings of relief and I felt more in control of the whole situation." When we asked him what was the chief benefit, he replied, "What I valued most was the feeling of acceptance. There was no judgement, my coach gave me the feeling that she was just there and, what is more, just for me."

CASE STUDY: 'TAKING THE BRAKES OFF'

Sabine received a call from the HR department of a major professional service firm with details of a new coaching client. The HR Director explained that the client was managing one of the organization's large projects and needed to learn to sell more, was possibly a candidate for promotion and potential partner material but was 'difficult' as a person.

A couple of days later Jim called and arranged to meet. He was very well prepared and presented all project evaluations and the results of a psychometric test from a recent training event. It was clear that he was eager to talk about how to sell more and get the whole process over and done with.

Sabine asked questions to slow him down and encourage reflection on his current situation. They talked about what was good about his career to date, what he enjoyed in life and what mattered most to him. What emerged was that none of the really satisfying and important things, events and situations in his life were career related. Somehow this was a real revelation to him as he had worked a 60+ hour week for the last four years. In addition, it became apparent to him that he had not yet made a clear decision about becoming a partner of the firm.

He abhorred his current lifestyle as a consultant and had aspirations to have a family of two children and a real home. Working long hours had recently been the final straw which led to the breakdown of a long-term relationship. Although achievement and progression meant a lot to him, against this backdrop he was really unsure whether going for promotion was the best choice for him.

Sabine and Jim spent three sessions talking about different scenarios, developing and evaluating options and initiating concrete action to improve his quality of life. As a result he became more relaxed and at ease with other people. He received more positive feedback from his team and clients than before. It was noticeable that he became more at ease with himself and empathetic in his communication style.

After becoming clear about his options and the impact they would have on his life he decided to go for promotion. Sabine and Jim worked on honing the goal and his 'personal brand' as a consultant. Once the goal was clear all the complex application documentation was developed within a short space of time and he started to position himself so that he could sell on and work on developing proposals for new clients.

Thus, it was clear that this was not about teaching somebody how to sell professional services, rather what was lacking was a focus and the decision to go for promotion within the firm. Making the decision really helped Jim to 'take the brakes off' and get on with both his professional and personal life.

SUMMARY: ASSESSING THE CURRENT SITUATION

This stage of the Achieve process is principally about allowing the executive to take time for deep reflection about his current position and issues that he is facing. Consequently this chapter has shown how to:

- lay the foundations of trust for a coaching relationship
- understand the issues, situation and the context of the client
- understand and identify development areas
- identify the most critical development issues
- understand the world from the point of view of the client

Top tips include:

- allow for and be able to endure 'silence'
- allow a process of co-discovery
- explore the context
- show empathy
- 'triangulate' to discover the executive's real needs

CHAPTER ELEVEN Step 2: Creative brainstorming of alternatives

ELEVEN Step 2: Creative brainstorming of alternatives

General description

This phase of executive coaching widens the executive's perspective and creates a sound foundation for the development of creative solutions and behavioural change. One of the objectives of coaching is to increase the choices that a client has when approaching a challenge or specific situation.

From our experience, and through talking to other executive coaches, it is clear that one of the most common pressing issues for clients is the feeling of being 'stuck' in a particular situation with no clear alternative course of action. In some circumstances, particularly in times of heightened stress, our perspective can narrow and we experience mental, physical and emotional 'tunnel vision'. It is rather like standing in front of a monumental wall and not being able to see anything other than the wall. Experienced executive coaches pull the client away from the wall so that they have a wider perspective again.

This wider perspective is a helpful prerequisite for the next stages in the coaching programme. We have found that this state is important as otherwise the client keeps on circling and repeating the same patterns of behaviour. Essentially the first natural reaction in a specific situation is doing 'more of the same'.

However, as the old saying goes, if you keep on doing what you have always done – you will keep on getting what you have always got. This situation can hardly be satisfactory for a client. It is the role of the executive coach to challenge the thinking, shake up the perspectives and assist the client 'to get out of the rut' and generate new options that can lead to new forms of behaviour.

The objectives

The objectives of this stage are to:

- assist the client to get out of the 'stuck state'
- assist the client to get into a 'solution state'
- assist the client to create a solid platform to think about alternatives

Why is it so difficult to get out of the stuck state on our own? This question probably has as many answers as there are people in stuck states. However, in our executive coaching experience we have had clients give us answers ranging from, "It felt safe – I didn't have to take risks with something new" to "I just couldn't see another way of doing things."

One explanation may be connected with the way in which we select information from the 'data storm' that is bombarding us every second. Approximately 2,000,000 bits of information are coming at us every second. However, the human brain can only process 134 bits per second.

So, we can only focus on a tiny percentage of information about the world around us. To guard against data overload we have developed a series of filters which direct our focus and determine the way in which we make sense of the world. The filters include our attitudes, values and beliefs, memories, previous decisions, our typical patterns of behaviour and how we interpret language that is used.

The filters develop over time and are determined by our experiences. The operation of these filters explains why we tend to keep on doing the same thing over and over again rather than seeking new pathways.

Getting the client out of a 'stuck state' can simply be helping him to recognize that he keeps running the same patterns of behaviour over and over again without getting the desired result. For others, the catalyst may be an increased awareness of the consequences of habitual patterns. Our coaching practice, however, has shown us that it may also be that they cannot think of alternative ways of doing things.

These alternatives are not 'solutions' nor need they be directly connected with the current situation. The key is that the client is seeking an alternative outcome so it is important to help him to have a basis that provides him with a wider perspective and puts him in a frame of mind to develop goals.

With one client, who talked of frustration with her boss's apparent inability to understand that speaking on the telephone to her rather than emailing would produce better results, we observed that the executive coach focused on working with the executive to produce a list of different scenarios. One of them involved the executive running a small hotel (not the current role at all). Another involved achieving promotion within the current organization and another involved a reorganization of the team structure. All presented alternatives to the current frustrating situation but none of them sought to provide solutions to the minutiae of the apparent problem.

What became clear is that the role of the executive coach in this stage is to help the client to accept personal responsibility for change and to recognize that they can only change their own behaviour, not that of others. So, to loop back to the previous example, if the coach had worked on ways the client could persuade the boss to use the telephone it would not have helped the client to think more broadly about the current situation and if the boss had refused to change, the frustrations would have remained. By not focusing on the issue of the telephone the coach was helping the client to broaden her options altogether and then develop desired goals that are really meaningful to her.

Key behaviours of experienced executives coaches

• Applies a variety of tools and techniques to take the client away from his habitual patterns and break his 'stuck state'
• Surprises clients with creative questions he does not expect at this stage
• Takes time to brainstorm about real alternatives to the current situation
• Probes beyond client's initial responses to uncover a broad spectrum of alternatives to the current situation

Table 2: Key behaviours of experienced executive coaches in creative brainstorming

Top tips

- **Release tension with an unexpected question like 'The miracle question'**. This question stems from solution focused therapy and can be asked in a number of ways, one version is "Suppose that one night, while you are asleep, there is a miracle and the problem you are facing is solved. However, because you are asleep you don't know that the miracle has already happened. When you wake up in the morning, what will be different that will tell you that the miracle has taken place? What else?" For many clients this provides the trigger which helps them begin to see new ways forward.
- **Use metaphorical tales**. Some executive coaches use metaphors to assist the client out of a stuck state. The tales or stories should be carefully designed to elicit a series of states. A state is the sum total of all neurological and physical processes within an individual at any moment in time, e.g. the state of excitement in the client which will be helpful to him as he moves forward. The great advantage of adopting this approach is that by adopting a 'story-telling mode' the coach immediately helps the client to relax and hence be in a better state to develop new solutions. Using a story can influence the client without being directive. Visual metaphors can also be useful. One executive coach we observed made good use of the office surroundings and began talking about the pot plants on the table. The plants were clearly in need of nutrients – they had yellowing leaves and were wilting. By talking about the plants the coach guided the client towards assessing his own needs and the constraints of his environment and role.
- **Visioning**. We have found that this technique can be used effectively to produce a series of pictures or statements that describe where the person wants to be, based on the high points of their life to date. As these pictures and/or statements are grounded in real experience and history people understand how to repeat their success. For example, remembering a past success in a job interview when preparing for the next career move. In essence the executive coach is awakening an old, but at present a latent, resource within the client.

From the client's perspective

From the client's perspective one of the most common reactions at this stage is one of surprise at the catalytic effect of interrupting a pattern. One said that "The question really made me think. I hadn't thought before that if I changed then it has a 'domino effect' on everyone else around me."

Other reactions were that they really appreciated being able to view the issue they were facing from an entirely different perspective. By thinking about alternatives rather than trying to solve a problem one individual said that this, "...somehow freed up my thinking." He elaborated on this and explained that the moment he was able to laugh about the whole situation in the coaching session he realized that he could get a grip on the situation.

CASE STUDY: 'THE PUBLIC SERVANT ON STAGE'

John was a newly appointed Director in a large public sector organization. Part of his role involved speaking to large, often hostile, audiences to introduce new aspects of government policy. He was seeking help from an executive coach as he found these events caused him to become over defensive and aggressive towards his audience. His defensive behaviour led him to bluster and try to shout down any resistance in the audience. He knew he did not want to continue with this pattern of behaviour as he felt, and was getting feedback from others, that it made him lose the confidence of his stakeholders and appear less than professional.

At first John could only see two alternatives: 1. to stop making presentations altogether and delegate them to a public servant in his team who seemed to be able to build good audience rapport even when delivering bad news, or 2. to carry on and hope that practise would improve his technique. Realistically he knew that the first alternative was not really an option, his position dictated that he was the one to deliver the message. The second alternative really made him wonder whether he was in the right job.

John was falling into the all too common trap of just wanting to put more effort into something which was not producing results, rather than trying something new.

To stimulate new thinking Fiona first took John outside away from his offices. As they walked it was clear that he was starting to relax. Fiona asked him what his ideal conference performance would be. He described it very clearly – confident, in control, getting audience participation and people coming up at the end to thank him for an enjoyable and productive day. Fiona was struck by the clarity of his description of a great stage performance. How did he know this so clearly? It emerged that this was something he had done before in a non-work context at his local amateur dramatic club.

Reminding himself of this experience was the starting point to stimulate John to think about alternatives to his current situation. They sat on the grass and John began writing furiously on a large piece of paper. Soon he had a list of new ideas, some of which are listed below:

1. Hold small local group meetings rather than one large conference
2. Send people briefing papers before the meeting so that they come prepared and 'forewarned'
3. Spend more time getting to know individuals by seeing them in their home offices on a one to one basis to build relationships
4. Hold weekly online 'surgeries' to allow people to air their issues

Some of these are more closely related to the original issue than others – the common thread is that they all represent different ways John could communicate with his audience.

In the next sessions they went on to clarify exactly what John was trying to achieve and to detail the ways in which he was going to take action.

Now John still has to deliver tough messages but, as a result of the work that we did together in the coaching sessions, he approaches the task with far less trepidation and has a much expanded repertoire of options for getting his message across whilst allowing others to have their say.

SUMMARY: CREATIVE BRAINSTORMING OF ALTERNATIVES

This phase of the Achieve Coaching Model® is focused on widening the executive's perspective and creating a solid foundation for the development of creative solutions and behavioural change. The main goal of brainstorming here is to increase the range of choices that the client has ahead of the development of specific goals and solutions.

This chapter has shown how to:

- assist the client to get out of the 'stuck state'
- assist the client to get from a problem or deficiency state into a 'solution state'
- assist the client to think about alternatives
- begin to map out the outlines of the desired new state with the client

Top tips include:

- release tension with an unexpected question
- use metaphorical tales
- deploy visioning techniques to broaden the client's perspective

CHAPTER TWELVE Step 3: Honing goals

TWELVE Step 3: Honing goals

General description

This is the third stage within the Achieve Coaching Model®. Having established alternatives to the current situation and a rough idea about the desired new state, the next step is to refine this into a specific goal. It is the stage where SMART goals are created and/or refined.

It is essential that the principles for the formulation of goals are taken into account. This is not as easy as it looks at first sight. Most executives are very aware of what they do not want. However, they frequently find it highly challenging to specify exactly what they do want. This stage is about helping the executive to articulate clearly what he wants.

The objectives

The objectives of this stage are:

- assist the executive to develop and/or hone his specific goal(s)
- ensure that the chosen goal is of high personal relevance
- help the executive to focus on the goal

At the beginning of the executive coaching programme most executives, in our experience, have direction for their career and/or the coaching programme but have seldom articulated their goal precisely in a SMART style. It may also have been some time since the executive really took time to reflect and think about what they actually want to achieve. In an executive coaching context this can mean that the client may need to create a goal from scratch or to refine one that is, at this stage, too vague and not well articulated.

In the core capability section we highlighted the importance of choosing a goal which has high personal relevance for the client. From our own experience, and from observing other executive coaches in action, we cannot over emphasize this point. Working with a client on a goal which is not relevant is likely to be a very unrewarding experience and it is unlikely to yield sustainable results for the client or the organization. It is therefore important to check that the goal is important on a personal level to the client, and not just to the organization or some significant other.

Having established and refined the goal it then serves as a focal point for future sessions. The coach's role is then to ensure that this goal is still important to the client as the programme progresses.

Key behaviours of experienced executive coaches

• Encourages precise definition of goals in positive terms
• Takes time to develop SMART, PURE, CLEAR goals
• Works with the client to develop goal(s) with high personal meaning and relevance
• Develops clear measures with client so that he can have evidence of achievement of the goal

Table 3: Key behaviours of experienced executive coaches in honing goals

Top tips

- **Use all five senses to build complete representation of the achievement of the goal.** Ask questions about how it will look, feel, sound etc. when the client has achieved his goal. This helps the executive gain clarity about the goal and its personal relevance. It provides a mental rehearsal which enables the client to check this is what he really wants. Further defining the goal in sensory terms, the goal becomes even more appealing and acts as a compelling magnet for the client.
- **Use questions to check personal relevance of goal.** By asking the following series of questions the coach can challenge the executive

and encourage them to consider the consequences of their plans from all angles.

- What will happen if you achieve the goal?
- What will not happen if you achieve the goal?
- What will happen if you do not achieve the goal?
- What will not happen if you do not achieve the goal?

From the client's perspective

A common theme we identified in the interviews with clients is that goal setting is quite often experienced as one of the most challenging phases in the whole executive coaching process. One client told us that, "This was the most difficult part of the whole coaching experience. I found it really hard to articulate what I wanted. When we explored this it became clear to me that I have always managed to be successful in my life. Now I'm at a crossroads in my career and it became clear to me that I've avoided setting goals as I've already got much further than I thought I would, and was scared to identify the next step. A failure would have questioned my identity as an achiever. We explored what held me back and the factors that always drove me forward. It took me the time in between the coaching sessions to come to terms with it and then we managed to develop new goals that really matter to me."

Another client described the impact of this stage as, "I could not believe how hard this part was. There I was used to defining clear revenue and sales targets for my teams and really struggling to define my own goals. I felt pathetic and also realized that I stopped having real goals years ago. Somehow I just worked and worked and worked."

Another theme that emerged is the new pride that clients found in having goals again and the realization that it frees up new energy and that the goals act like a 'magnet' and or 'beacon'. "I was amazed how much energy I still have and work has become really quite exciting again: my new goals draw me in the right direction and things just started to happen and all in the right direction."

CASE STUDY: 'DISTILLING THE ESSENCE OF DESIRE'

Anwar came to coaching with a clear desire. At his very first session he said, "I need to be more strategic". Clear enough, but what did that actually mean and how would he know when he had achieved it? Anwar had recently been promoted to the board of directors of a pharmaceutical company and was widely acknowledged to be a good manager and a good technical specialist. However, he was less certain of what it meant to be a good director and even more confused when people started to refer to him as a leader in the organization.

Fiona worked with Anwar to help him clarify his goal and to formulate it in a way which meant he could take practical steps towards achieving it. The first step was to ascertain what he meant by strategic. Fiona asked him how he would behave differently if he was acting strategically. The purpose of this question was to help both of them understand what he was trying to achieve in order to arrive at a shared understanding. Anwar said that if he were acting strategically then he would be less involved in the hands-on delivery of a project and more involved in thinking about the general direction and expected outcomes. So he saw himself as the one who would decide what the department's priorities would be and then leave others to think about the detail of how these would be achieved. As he talked it became clear to Anwar that at present he was stuck in the operational aspects of the job. However, what he was aiming for was to improve his delegation skills and to learn to let go of the day-to-day working on a project.

Anwar reformulated his goal as: "I will have delegated three projects by the end of October and will have set up regular weekly reporting meetings with each of the three managers". In the next meetings they then proceeded to work on how and what to delegate and Anwar's options for achieving his goal.

The time released through delegation has given Anwar the time to think about the strategic direction of the organization and to develop his skills as a director of the organization.

SUMMARY: HONING GOALS

The third stage of the Achieve Coaching Model® focuses on refining the desired end state developed by the client and executive coach into specific goals.

This chapter has shown how to:

- assist the executive to develop and/or hone goals
- uncover if the chosen goal is of high personal relevance
- help the client to focus on the goal

Top tips include:

- use all five senses to build a complete picture of the end goals and the resources required to achieve the goals
- use questions to check the personal relevance of the goals

CHAPTER THIRTEEN Step 4: Initiating options

THIRTEEN Step 4: Initiating options

General description

This is the fourth step of the Achieve Coaching Model®. Having decided upon a specific goal, the aim at this stage is to develop a wide range of different ways of achieving the executive's desired goal. The purpose at this stage is not to find the 'right' option but to stimulate the executive to develop a great array of options for achieving his goal. It is important to encourage the executive to get off the 'beaten track'.

No option, however seemingly appealing, should form the sole focus of attention at this stage. The executive must be encouraged and stimulated to consider a broad spectrum of options. The quantity, novelty and variety of the options is, at this stage, more important than the quality and feasibility.

Experienced executive coaches appear to leverage know-how from creative process techniques. At this stage it is particularly important that the executive feels comfortable and that there is a relaxed and, above all, judgement free atmosphere. It may even be appropriate to conduct these sessions away from the normal meeting place as this can add another stimulus to thinking off the 'beaten track'.

In some sessions we observed the coach encouraging the executive to combine and refine the options based on the techniques of 'piggybacking' – that is, to combine two or more options to generate a previously unimagined option.

It is essential that as many as possible of the options are generated by the executive. However, if the coach has experience in this specific area and, in the discussion, ideas for options emerge he should note them down. What we have seen with experienced executive coaches is that they do not just add these in to the conversation, rather they make a clear statement of an offer, e.g. "This relates to a past experience I have, do you want to hear what this was and how it worked?" The expertise of the executive coach is used but he asks for permission to contribute before entering into the discussion. The coach can contribute but it is crucial that the executive develops ownership of the option – the executive coach is just the guide through the process.

The objectives

The objectives of this stage are to:

- develop a wide range of (behavioural) options
- encourage the executive to go off the 'beaten track', i.e. outside his normal range of behaviours

We have seen executive coaches who employ the full range of creative techniques from paradigm preserving to paradigm breaking. The range of creative techniques is detailed in Figure 11 below.

	PARADIGM PRESERVING	PARADIGM STRETCHING	PARADIGM BREAKING
Problem boundaries	Unchanged	Stretched	Broken
Creative stimulation	Low	Medium	High
Stimuli	Related	Unrelated	Unrelated
Association	Free	Forced	Forced
Expression	Verbal/Written	Verbal/Written	Unlimited
Examples of CPS	Brainstorming Brainwriting	Object Stimulation Metaphors	Wishful Thinking Rich Pictures
Techniques	Force Field Analysis World Diamond	Assumption Reversal	Picture Stimulation Collage

Figure 11: The Creativity Continuum

Source: Adapted from McFadzean E.S. (1999), Creativity in MS/OR: Choosing the appropriate technique, Interfaces, Vol 29, No.5, pp110-22

One technique that we have experienced in action ourselves with an excellent result is object stimulation. Here the executive is asked to describe an object and use the descriptions as an unrelated stimulus to encourage the development of novel options. In one session we experienced an executive who chose his coffee mug as the object he wanted to describe. Initially the descriptions focused on readily observable features such as shape and colour. He then went on to describe its everyday use. The executive coach was largely silent but probed on certain descriptions. The executive then suddenly began listing a whole range of alternative uses for the mug. He then experienced an 'aha! moment' and said, "I see where this is going. I limit myself by focusing on the obvious." He went on to generate fresh options for using his time and leveraging the skills of his team. Object stimulation can be effective stimulation for clients to leave their 'beaten track' by using unrelated stimuli and forced association.

Carefully crafted metaphors can also be useful at this stage to stimulate thinking about new options. We have found that metaphors are most effectively used in an executive coaching context when the following four steps are considered and carefully taken into account:

- displace the focus of attention from the client to a character in a story
- link to the client's issue by establishing behaviours and events between the characters in the story that are similar to those in the client's situation
- suggest ideas for the client to consider within the context of the story
- conclude the story so that a sequence of events occurs in which the characters in the story resolve the conflict and achieve the desired outcome

One executive coach described how he uses rich pictures as part of his coaching programme. He encourages the executive to draw a picture of the future and a picture of the present situation. He then explores both pictures and the paths running from present to future, thus encouraging the executive to think of new ways of moving from present to future.

In our study we found more examples on the left side of the creativity continuum (see Figure 11) than on the right side. This may be the result of a variety of causes including the training and background of the executive coaches. The skilful use of paradigm stretching and paradigm breaking techniques will require in-depth training. In many executive coaching training programmes these techniques are either not covered at all or not in any depth to develop expertise in this area. It may also be that the whole reflective process of executive coaching in combination with some creative techniques may be sufficient to yield the desired results. However, it is a skill that we believe can be further exploited in executive coaching.

Key behaviours of experienced executive coaches

• Exhibits confidence in the process and works with the client to develop alternative pathways to arriving at the desired goal
• Uses a broad spectrum of questioning styles and other techniques to stimulate the client to generate options
• Provides space and time for the client to develop a range of options
• Ensures that the options are the client's and he has real ownership

Table 4: Key behaviours of experienced executive coaches in initiating options

Top tips

- **Self-generation of options**. You have to remember that the key aim of executive coaching is to get the client to help themselves. If you rush in to provide new strategies you are laying the foundations for problems later. As one experienced executive coach said to us, "What I mean is, that you have to resist helping, if you help now then you limit the possibilities for the executive for the future and they don't take responsibility for generating solutions – you set up a dependency. If you have an idea that is valid the best thing is to clearly label it as such and then get them to build upon it."
- **Trust in the process**. It is very important to exhibit patience and resist the temptation to rush ahead. Sometimes it can seem hard but you just have to stay quiet. Those pauses are vital to allow the client to come up with new options and to take responsibility for their future actions.

From the client's perspective

When we talked about this stage to clients it became clear that the ease of generating new options varied from client to client. One said, "Once I was clear about what I wanted to achieve, thinking about various ways to actually get there was not that hard. Although the challenge was to think outside of my own box..." We have encountered this quite often in our own coaching practice. The initial thoughts for alternative options are more often than not within the narrow frame of existing behavioural patterns.

However, 'more of the same' does not usually get the executive to the desired goal. As the old saying goes if you do what you have always done, you get what you have always got. Thus, encouragement and creative questioning techniques are critical to ensure that thinking outside the box can take place and new behavioural options can be developed.

Another theme we identified in our study and found mirrored with our own client base is that without the coaching sessions the executive can get lost in day-to-day activities, and simply does not find time and space to think of new options. As one said, "I felt safe in the situation and we managed to come up with lots of ideas about how I could approach this. It was really liberating. It is not that I can't do this, it is simply that I don't take the time – I somehow tend to be on autopilot and run the usual programme."

We also identified that this stage is experienced as a relief by some executives. One who was previously circling without achieving what he actually wanted said, "It's a relief, I can now see that I actually have quite a few options going forward."

CASE STUDY: 'STAR OF INDIA'

For Natasha it had become clear that life in the Public Sector was not for her. Her strong affiliation to her Indian heritage had led her to dream of living in India and working with the women and girls in the area around her parents' original home village. She wanted to increase the accessibility of education and opportunity. Her passion for this was undeniable but she had not thought about ways of making her dream into a reality. She had allowed self-doubt, and the vision of the many practical barriers that could arise, to keep her dream as something that might happen 'one day'.

Natasha decided to use our executive coaching sessions to work on taking the first steps towards achieving her dream. It was too big a goal to simply leave England and set up a school in India. As one of the main practical barriers was finance, the goal of the coaching became alternative careers for Natasha which would enable her to generate sufficient income to put aside money for investment in her ultimate goal.

To initiate options Fiona first asked Natasha to list her skills and also her interests outside of the work context.

The lists she produced were:

Skills

- Project management
- Good with people
- Presentation skills
- Writing skills
- PR
- Budget monitoring
- Planning
- Attention to detail
- Good at explaining things
- Leading a team

Interests

- Indian vegetarian cooking
- Interior design (she had helped many friends set up flats and had given the family home a complete makeover)
- Voluntary work with children
- Religion: Community groups associated with the temple
- Self-development: Courses on self-hypnosis and regression
- Socializing with friends: Organizing parties and going to restaurants

Once she had completed the lists the next step in the process was to combine the skills and interests to produce some possible careers. By combining skills and interests in this way the aim was to both produce new ideas and also to try to ensure that whatever Natasha did next would provide a fulfilling career.

Natasha had not thought of doing this before and had been rather aimlessly looking at job adverts in newspapers. She produced a list of possible options for careers and after eliminating some the list was:

- Teacher
- Lecturer
- Counsellor
- Setting up and running an Indian vegetarian restaurant
- Event organizer
- Journalist
- House doctor

Natasha's next step was to produce a list of criteria against which to evaluate each of the options. By using this list she was able to see where her priorities lay and is now working towards setting up her own Indian restaurant.

This case also illustrates the tensions that can exist between the three partners of the coaching relationship: organization, coach and client. As the coach is paid by the organization it could seem that working on an exit strategy for the client is at odds with organizational aims. Therefore it is important that the organizational sponsors understand from the outset that one outcome of the changes effected by executive coaching may be that an individual decides to move on. In the case of this public service client this was clearly discussed prior to the assignments and the sponsoring client agreed that he accept the outcome.

SUMMARY: INITIATING OPTIONS

The fourth stage of the Achieve Coaching Model® helps the client develop options to meet the goals established in the previous step. The broader the spectrum of options generated and considered the better. Thinking off the 'beaten track' must be encouraged by the executive coach.

This chapter has shown how to:

- develop a wide range of behavioural options
- encourage the executive to get off the 'beaten track', i.e. outside the normal range of behaviours

Top tips include:

- use metaphorical tales to introduce new angles of insight
- deploy tools to help the client self generate options
- trust the process to produce viable options – give it time to work

CHAPTER FOURTEEN Step 5: Evaluate options

FOURTEEN Step 5: Evaluate options

General description

Having generated a comprehensive list of options, the next stage is to evaluate the options systematically and prioritize them for the action plan. After goal setting this is the next stage where the coach can guide the executive towards developing focus. In our study and our own international coaching practice we experienced that developing focus for the executive was essential in the midst of the complexities of his day-to-day life and responsibilities. Without a well-defined focus for action the executive was unlikely to move forward effectively.

We have found that executives who are skilled at evaluating options for business objectives often find it difficult to apply the same techniques to their personal development. The executive is well aware of the techniques but does not readily translate these to his own plans. The executive coach serves to remind the executive of his skill and encourages him to apply it to his own personal situation.

The objectives

The objectives of this stage are to:

- identify a list of criteria against which the options can be evaluated
- evaluate the options against the criteria
- identify priorities

The criteria must be identified by the executive – the exact nature of the criteria will, of course, depend upon the situation/issue which is being addressed through coaching. Having elicited the criteria they may then be put into a matrix.

Once the matrix has been developed the client is then asked to evaluate each option using a point system of one to five where one is low and five is high. Once all options have been assessed all the numbers are added up and a total is calculated: the option with the highest number receives top priority.

	Evaluation criterion 1	Evaluation criterion 2	Evaluation criterion 3	**TOTAL**
Option 1				
Option 2				
Option 3				

The use of a matrix is just one way in which the options can be evaluated. We have also seen coaches guide an executive through the process using a force field analysis technique.

Force field analysis is a method for listing, discussing and evaluating the various forces for and against a proposed change. When a change is planned, force field analysis helps you look at the big picture by analyzing all of the forces impacting the change and weighing up the pros and cons. By knowing the pros and cons, you can develop strategies to reduce the impact of the opposing forces and strengthen the supporting forces.

- Forces that help you achieve the change are called 'driving forces'
- Forces that work against the change are called 'restraining forces'
- Force field analysis can be used to develop an action plan to implement a change. Specifically it can …
  - determine if a proposed change can get needed support
  - identify obstacles to successful solutions
  - suggest actions to reduce the strength of the obstacles

The choice of technique will depend on the preferred style of the executive and his coach. However, whatever the outcome of employing these techniques the final choice is the result of the overall coaching conversation. The techniques are just meant to support the discussion.

Having evaluated a number of options it may be that the executive decides to pursue more than one. The next step is therefore to decide on the order in which they will take forward the options in the plan. Although the priorities should be set by the executive, the coach can guide the process by asking questions such as "Which of these options, if you followed it through, would have the greatest impact on your current situation?"

We have found that it is useful for the executive to keep a written record of the evaluation stage so that decisions can be reviewed in the light of changing circumstances.

Key behaviours of experienced executive coaches

• Encourages the client to develop his own criteria for the evaluation of options
• Ensures real ownership of the evaluation criteria as these form the basis on which options are chosen or rejected
• Takes time to probe client to develop a full evaluation of each option
• Ensures that the key options and their evaluation are fixed in writing for future reference

Table 5: Key behaviours of experienced executive coaches in evaluating options

Top tips

- **Use a structured points system to help the client evaluate the options**. By awarding points to each of the options against a set of criteria the client gets a clearer view of the relative strengths and weaknesses of each of the alternative options.
- **Ensure that the evaluation table is written down for future reference**. It is really important to get the client's commitment to action. In addition, some clients put the plan up in a prominent place so that they have a reminder of the basis on which they made their decisions.

From the client's perspective

Going through a systematic approach to evaluation can be time consuming. One client described his frustrations, "I found it tedious to go through this phase. For me it was clear which option I wanted to take. I didn't want to fluff around and wanted to 'go for it'. However, the irony of it was that 'just going for it' was actually the theme we were working on. I acted too often without thinking about the consequences."

A common theme that emerged from our client feedback interviews was that at the end of the coaching assignment they perceived it as extremely valuable to have developed alternative options, evaluated them and therefore be in a position to make a conscious choice for a specific option. A client described it as "Tremendous value to go through this ... It has given me the confidence that the options chosen are really the right ones. I have come back on several occasions to the notes from that session." This also provides further evidence of how important it is for the client to make and keep sound written records of the sessions.

CASE STUDY: 'FINDING THE PERFECT MATCH'

Sue's Business Unit underwent a review by the American parent organization. At the end of the review they decided to close the Business Unit in Europe. A few managers would receive an offer to join other parts of the business but the majority had to leave and were offered severance packages. Sue was one of the fortunate few who were given the chance to move to another part of the organization in a different city. She felt deeply hurt and humiliated through the whole process and decided to privately seek the assistance of an executive coach to work with her on developing options and moving ahead.

Sue wanted to concentrate on developing her professional goal. She told Sabine that by the age of 42 she wanted to be a General Manager of an organization. This meant she had another four years to achieve her professional goal and would need one to two career moves in between to gain the necessary experience. Her first step was to prepare a new CV and to talk to head-hunters about potential options for her in the current market. Within a couple of weeks two potential positions in new organizations were offered to her.

However, at the next coaching session Sue was adamant that remaining with her current organization was actually the best option. She explained that she was not absolutely certain and that she was probably also slightly scared to leave and prove herself all over again in a new environment. To help her make the best choice for herself Sabine challenged her to develop a set of evaluation criteria against which she would be able to assess the various options. Sabine asked her to write up the evaluation criteria on a white board. For the next step Sabine asked her to evaluate each option in relation to each criterion on a scale from 1-10, where 1 is low and 10 is high.

Here is the list that was developed in the coaching session:

Criteria	**Organization A**	**Organization B**	**Organization C**
Chances to become a General Manager	8	6	8
The job	4	8	8
Professional development	8	4	5
Quality of life	6	6	5
Location	7	9	1
Hierarchical level	4	9	5
Compensation	6	5	9
'Glamour of business world'	8	4	9
Fun	8	3	6
Professional risks	8	2	5
Total	**67**	**56**	**61**
Ranking	**1**	**3**	**2**

When Sue saw the table she was surprised at the outcome. Organization C was her current organization and yet was not number one on the list. When she started to reflect she noticed that she had been blinded by the size of the compensation package in combination with the glamour factor of the business. Other factors such as professional development took a back seat. She had also only seen the immediate, short-term benefits and not considered the impact on her long-term career progression.

She was surprised about how close she had come to making a 'wrong' decision. She was very used to evaluating options in business but had never thought of applying the same techniques to personal decisions. She lived with the results until the next session when she explained that it had really started to sink in and make sense. Now Sue is with organization A and very happy with her choice.

SUMMARY: EVALUATE OPTIONS

Executive coaches who are able to assist the client in the systematic evaluation of options are highly valued in the market place. The process whereby the client is helped to assess and select his preferred options for action can be a powerful way to reinforce commitment to achieving change.

The chapter has shown how to:

- identify a list of criteria against which the options can be evaluated
- evaluate the options against the criteria
- identify priorities

Top tips include:

- use a structured points system to help the client evaluate the options
- make sure the evaluation table is written down for future reference

CHAPTER FIFTEEN Step 6: Valid action programme design

FIFTEEN Step 6: Valid action programme design

General description

At this stage a concrete and pragmatic action plan is designed or, as one coach described, "It is where the rubber meets the road!" We experience over and over again that one of the main reasons why executive coaching is valued in industry and commerce is that it provides 'just in time' learning and development. This stage of committing to a plan means that the executive is starting on the road to action.

With many executive development programmes the challenge is how to translate the 'classroom learning' back into everyday practice. Executive coaching helps bridge the gap and commits the executive to taking action with newly acquired skills.

Valid action programme design is not something that just occurs at the end of the coaching programme. Throughout the process the coach will be assisting the executive to plan and to take concrete action in his everyday life.

As the end of the executive coaching engagement approaches it is useful for the executive to have a plan for the period after the coach has left. In this way, designing a plan can be seen as part of the preparation for closure – the ending of the coaching relationship. Executive coaching is designed to be a short-term intervention which does not create dependency.

The objectives

The main objectives at this stage are to:

- gain commitment to action
- identify concrete actions and/or exercises that help an executive to progress towards his goal

We identified that almost all experienced executive coaches insist on gaining the executive's commitment to specific actions at the end of a coaching session. As a US coach explained to us, "The face to face meetings are staging posts ... the real development and progress happens in between the coaching sessions."

The agreed actions and/or exercises can have various objectives such as to:

- get things done on the job
- expand the executive's existing networks
- learn more about personal aspects
- experiment with alternative behaviours to widen the behavioural repertoire
- gain insights about what is working. What are the contributing factors?
- gain insights into what is not working. What are the contributing factors?

All too often the initial steps for a change in behaviour can be seen as too large and therefore the client feels overwhelmed and takes no action. Breaking a large goal into small achievable action steps can make it less overwhelming to take the first step. Small steps add up and build towards the achievement of the critical milestones and the milestones add up to the achievement of the larger goal. By taking and achieving small action steps and getting feedback of success the client gains motivation to keep going forward.

Key behaviours of experienced executive coaches

• Creates a detailed action plan with the client
• Works with the client to check the reality and achievability of the plan
• Fixes action plan in writing
• Ensures commitment to the action plan

Table 6: Key behaviours of experienced executive coaches in valid action programme design

Top tips

- **Detail exactly what is needed to achieve the desired goal, what the potential barriers are, what resources are needed for implementation, and the due dates.** One of the reasons executives do not achieve their goals is that they have not taken time out to plan and consider exactly what they need to do, potentially differently, to achieve it. A detailed action plan provides transparency and allows for checking along the way.
- **Make sure the client writes down the detailed action plan.** This provides visible evidence of the commitment to taking action as well as serving as an *aide memoire* for the steps to be taken. By referring back to the action plan the client can also recognize and celebrate achievements.
- **Co-create small action steps that form an integral part of the overall action plan at the end of each session.** This provides a tangible outcome on a continuous basis during the executive coaching programme and creates momentum. In addition, it enhances the confidence of the executive to achieve his goal through his own actions.
- **Review progress and renew commitment to the action plan in each session.** This ensures momentum and provides reassurance. By noting progress to date and challenging and overcoming any barriers to success the executive coach helps keep the client on track towards the achievement of the overall goal.

From the client's perspective

From the client's perspective this stage often proves to be instrumental in making the commitment for a specific goal tangible and visible. As one female manager explained, "Up until then it had all been up in the air, 10ft above the ground and actually quite daunting. But writing it down did two things: it made it seem possible and it committed me to doing it. Now that it was in black and white I had to do it. It also was good that we devised concrete action steps which I could see would actually take me to my goal one step at a time. This was much more up my street."

Indeed this was a common theme emerging from conversations with clients. Throughout the coaching programme, conversations take place about many aspects of the client's behaviour and life. Sometimes this can leave the client wondering where the programme is going. By constructing concrete action steps the whole process becomes clear and clients can see how it all leads to action.

The steps taken to produce the plan can also be used to help keep the executive focused and on track. "When we started referring back to the action plan I started to realize how far I had actually already travelled. It boosted my confidence in my own action and this really fuelled my determination to keep going."

CASE STUDY: 'STEPPING INTO THE SPOTLIGHT'

Stuart had recently been appointed to the board of one of the top ten organizations in the country. In the first month he focused on understanding the organization, meeting the stakeholders and forming his team. He was known to be competent but had so far stayed out of the spotlight in the organization. Then, suddenly, he had to prepare for a major presentation at the company's annual meeting of the top 250 executives. As this was his first time in the spotlight he called for help to prepare for the meeting.

When he met Sabine and discussed the situation he soon started to realize that preparation for the 'Top 250 event' was only one aspect of his challenge – the major issue was, how to position himself, create an impact in the new organization and gain recognition for his unique personal contribution and abilities.

Sabine asked him what he would do to promote a new product and he began detailing the steps. Stuart then realized that he could apply a similar process to his presentation. They talked about first steps and Sabine suggested that a starting point would be to clarify his 'personal brand' and its attributes. What did he actually stand for in the organization? What did he wish to stand for in the organization? Once Stuart established his personal brand attributes, Sabine worked with him to co-create a detailed action plan leading up to the event.

Excerpt from Stuart's action plan:

Goal	Action steps	Potential barriers	Resources needed	Due date	Status
Develop a strong authentic personal brand with five core characteristics	Identify five core characteristics that are genuinely meaningful and authentic	Identify attributes that are socially desirable but not authentic	About two coaching sessions plus three x two hours dedicated personal time		
Create a sound experience of the personal brand	Identify the critical 'touch points', i.e. where the personal brand characteristics can be experienced	Create touch points which are not relevant for everyday experience	Dedicated time in coaching session		
Increase recognition in the organization	Create articles for the in-house magazine	Lack of newsworthy content	Board Assistant Internal Communication team		
	Develop a feature for the company TV	Lack of internal resources to assist in the development and placement of the material	Board Assistant Internal Communication Team Advertising Agency Film Production Company		

Goal	Action steps	Potential barriers	Resources needed	Due date	Status
Develop presentation for the annual event	Draft presentation	Lack of time due to day-to-day work pressure	Coach Internal Communication team Design Agency		
	Share draft presentation with key stakeholders	Lack of time on the part of the stakeholders	Secretary to book time in calendars of key stakeholders for review		
	Integrate their comments	Lack of quality comments	Board Assistant		

The action plan helped Stuart to prepare well for the event. At the event he was able to position himself well amongst his board colleagues and received excellent feedback. After the event, articles about him appeared in the internal executive magazine and he had regular appearances on the company TV. All of this helped him to position himself as a key member of the top team in the organization.

SUMMARY: VALID ACTION PROGRAMME DESIGN

This stage sees the executive coach and client work together to develop a pragmatic action plan that is realistic in its timings and broken down into honestly achievable chunks. The action plan is only valid if it is believed to be fully implementable by the client with the resources to hand.

This chapter has shown how to:

- gain commitment to action
- identify concrete actions and/or exercises that help an executive to progress towards his goal

Top tips include:

- detail exactly what is needed to achieve the desired goal, what the potential barriers are, what resources are needed for implementation, and the due dates
- make sure the client writes down the detailed action plan
- create together small action steps, that form an integral part of the overall action plan, at the end of each session
- review progress and renew commitment to the action plan in each session

CHAPTER SIXTEEN Step 7: Encouraging momentum

SIXTEEN Step 7: Encouraging momentum

General description

In the Achieve Coaching Model® this is represented as the final stage. However, while it is an important final step to assist the client to stay on track, the role of the executive coach in encouraging momentum is equally important between the coaching sessions.

As a US coach explained it is "...a crucial part of the process. Until the new behaviour becomes the new reality it remains difficult ... executives who are in the transformation process need encouragement and reinforcement." We have found that it is also important to reinforce even the smallest steps as this helps to build and maintain momentum and increase the level of confidence of the executive. Small action steps contribute to creating critical mass and to manifesting the desired goal. Sustainable change is easier to achieve with continuous reinforcement and encouragement.

However obvious it may seem to encourage clients to move forward, we have seen executive coaches in our study who do not take this step in a coaching relationship or do not consistently encourage the client. Our finding is again in line with a study by Lore International who found that nearly 40% of clients in their own survey reported that their coach did not follow up after each coaching session to check that they were making the desired progress.

Embedding new skills/capabilities

The need for external encouragement from the executive coach is related to the stages a person moves through as they first learn and then master a new capability. The diagram below (Figure 12) illustrates the four quadrants through which a client will pass when integrating new learning. Within each of the four quadrants the coach has a critical role to help keep the client moving forwards.

Unconscious incompetence

In this stage the client is unaware of what he does not know. To use an analogy of driving a car: when you are a child you take driving skills for granted. You have no idea of what the process involves and just assume that once you reach 17 you will be able to drive. After all, your parents can do it so what could be the challenge?

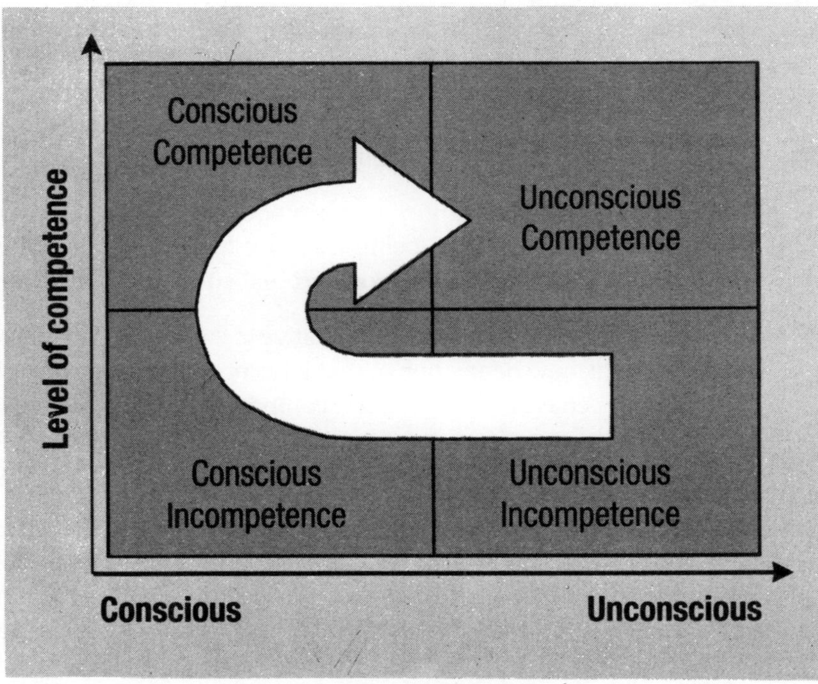

Figure 12: Embedding new skills/capabilities

In a coaching relationship it is the role of the coach to help the client uncover the hidden areas and to increase his level of self-awareness, as was highlighted in our description of the first stage of the Achieve Coaching Model®.

Conscious incompetence

The coaching process has assisted in creating awareness about the area for development. Now the client understands what they cannot do or what it is that they would like to do better.

Continuing the driving analogy – this is the first few lessons where you suddenly realize just how much there is to do to drive a car. How will you ever learn to co-ordinate hands, feet and eyes?

This stage can be unsettling in a coaching relationship particularly if the executive does not have patience. However, if their sense of urgency is high enough they will make the conscious decision to change and/or develop their skill/change their behaviour. The client needs to develop commitment to action to take them to the next level.

Conscious competence

At this stage the client knows what to do and how to do it but the process requires concentration and a conscious attention to detail.

In the trials of learning to drive, this stage is reached when you pass the test. Everything is still being done by the book – mirror, signal, manoeuvre. It takes concentration and real effort.

The coach needs to work with the executive to encourage him to continue to practise the new behaviour so that it becomes an integral part of the way that he behaves – unconscious competence.

Unconscious competence

At this level the executive has integrated the new skill and/or behaviour into their normal behaviour. Continuous practice and commitment leads to mastery.

Returning to the driving analogy: you are now driving confidently, almost on autopilot. Now you are on the 'hands-free' car phone and thinking about an upcoming meeting and driving – it can all be done simultaneously. Some days you can arrive at the office without being consciously awareness of the route you took or how you drove the car. This can be worrying and actually may be the spur to take your skill to the next level and begin the cycle of learning again.

At this stage the role of the executive coach is again to keep encouraging the client to keep him on track and broaden his learning.

The objectives

The objectives at this stage are to:

- assist the client to keep on track
- affirm positive action and results
- ensure that the goals of the coaching programme are achieved
- review progress

Experienced coaches highlight the importance of consistent follow-up. In practice we all know that it is not easy to follow a new goal in a focused manner as there are so many competing demands in everyday life. Nevertheless, to be an effective executive coach and help the client towards his objective it is important to devise a method of seeking and receiving regular updates.

Technological advances make the process much easier – now executive coaches can follow up by telephone, email and/or SMS as well as in person.

Encouragement and affirmation is particularly critical when the executive is in the process of making behavioural changes. As a rule of thumb the greater and/or the more critical the behavioural change, the more frequent the need for encouragement and affirmation.

Key behaviours of experienced executive coaches

• Demonstrates continuing interest in the development of the client
• Organizes regular 'checking in'/'keep on track'/'follow up' sessions in between coaching sessions
• Affirm positive action and results
• Knows when to end the relationship and takes measures throughout the coaching programme to avoid dependency

Table 7: Key behaviours of experienced executive coaches in ensuring momentum

Top tips

- **Encourage people to experiment with new behaviours for 21 days.** It has often been said that it takes 21 days to really change a habit. By keeping to a new pattern for 21 days the client has a greater chance of maintaining a new behaviour.
- **Choose areas for action and/or experimenting with new behaviours that feel safe and/or are really fun.** Clearly there are areas where it is more challenging to try out a new behaviour such as an important presentation or a critical client meeting. Other surroundings may be more comforting and thus it is easier to experiment, such as with family or in a circle of good friends. At the end of the day it is most critical that the executive starts to take the first step, tries out something new and thus creates a reference point for his new behaviour.
- **Use questions that are motivational in a real life context.** We have previously stated that many purchasers of coaching believe that the real value of the process lies in that it is 'just in time' and that, as executive coaches, we see that the real development and progress is made in between the sessions. Using questions such as, "What led you to do that? What were the factors in your decision? What could you do differently the next time?" can be very useful to help the executive to understand his driving energy, decision processes and priorities in a real life setting rather than in an artificial situation like a training room or even a coaching session. This is about real life!

From the client's perspective

Clients find little reminders and genuine encouragement for momentum very helpful. One client told us, "It was great, just when I was slipping back into my old ways I got a phone call. This really helped me to stay on track."

In fact, almost all clients described to us the challenges they faced in putting certain actions and behaviours they had committed to in the coaching session into practice. "It is really not that easy if you are used to doing things a certain way and you run your programme for years and then suddenly have to do it differently. I recognized really quickly that it was one thing to discuss my stuff in a coaching session and completely another to actually put it all into practice. More often than not I got lost in my usual day-to-day activities and doing the stuff the way I always did."

For coaches it is a useful reminder that clients have their individual needs and their preferences about the form of the encouragement of momentum in between the face-to-face coaching sessions and that technology now makes it possible that a variety of options are available. "I found brief SMS messages very helpful. They provided the little spark which was all I needed for a kick." Yet another client said, "What I found most helpful were our short telephone conversations early in the morning or at the end of the day. It really helped me a lot to stay on track."

Whereas another client commented, "When I leave home, sit in my car and I am on the way to work I found it tremendously helpful to talk things through. For a certain part of the programme we had weekly half hour telephone sessions. I would still say that I have achieved my desired goal due to these weekly telephone sessions. They were useful reminders and helped me to keep on track when I may have been tempted to fall back into old patterns."

CASE STUDY: 'KEEPING ON TRACK'

Mike is currently the Senior Vice President of a large global consumer goods company. His goal is to become a member of the board within two years. When Sabine began working with him he already had a mentor within the organization who was very valuable to him; providing advice and opening doors. It was important to incorporate this important resource into Mike's plans for achieving his goal. Sabine encouraged Mike to set up regular three-way communication between himself, his internal mentor and Sabine.

In the early part of the coaching programme a tightly structured personal development plan was created and signed off by the organization. Mike worked on his development with both his internal mentor and Sabine.

One of the issues was Mike's lack of focus and strategic direction. Due to his position in the organization he was invited to numerous meetings. Although he has an astute strategic mind he had a tendency to get lost in operational day-to-day activities and attended endless internal meetings, without assessing their value to his overall goal, as he felt he always should be present. When looking at his calendar weeks and weeks in advance it was clear that if no radical solution was found to cut the amount of meeting time, he would not find the time to incorporate critical activities and thinking time to develop strategic plans and reach the position on the board.

Sabine and Mike reviewed all the meetings and telephone conferences he had attended over the previous month and assessed the value of attending each of them against his goal. On the basis of the evaluation, Mike decided to delegate about 30% of the meetings to his direct reports and shorten other meetings by about 25%.

The time was saved through the implementation of a more focused meeting culture, i.e. he prepared an agenda for each meeting and ensured all attendees prepared for them so that time was used for discussion, sharing of experiences and decision making rather than for a review of figures that were written on PowerPoint slides. In all, the total time saved was over 12 hours per week!

Mike used this additional time for strategic thinking and the development of client relationships and further development of his team. Mike was delighted with the result but found it tough not to fall back into his old ways. He saw a need to change but his surroundings and the culture in the organizations was, of course, still the same. Mike recognized that this provided a big challenge and required stamina on his part to say "No" to many invitations and keep on track.

This was where Sabine's role in keeping him on track was vital. Mike found it helpful to receive short reminder SMSs and emails, and Sabine also scheduled brief weekly telephone conversations on his way to work early in the morning. At the end of the programme he felt that this encouragement was one of the major contributory factors for him achieving his goal.

Mike now has had feedback from the organization that he is clearly on track to become a board member. He attributes his success to three factors:

- partnering of internal mentor with external coach and open three-way conversations
- the structured and systematic coaching programme and
- Sabine's encouragement to keep him on track

SUMMARY: ENCOURAGING MOMENTUM

The final stage of the Achieve Coaching Model® is all about helping the client stay the course and reach their goals. Learning how to best encourage and support the client to maintain their momentum and commitment is a vital skill for the effective executive coach.

This chapter has shown how to:

- ensure that the goals of the coaching programme are achieved
- review progress effectively

Top tips include:

- encourage people to experiment with new behaviours for 21 days
- choose areas for action and/or experimenting with new behaviours that feel safe and/or are really fun
- use questions that are motivational

In this part we described in detail the seven steps of the Achieve Coaching Model®. By providing detailed descriptions and looking at each stage from various perspectives we aimed to make the executive coaching process more transparent and to contribute to the further development of effective and efficient coaching practice in organizations.

PART THREE OVERALL SUMMARY: THE ACHIEVE COACHING MODEL® – THE SYSTEMATIC APPROACH TO EFFECTIVE EXECUTIVE COACHING

From our international best practice study and analysis of existing models such as the GROW Model we identified that experienced effective executive coaches apply, consciously or unconsciously, a seven step process to achieve real results in coaching assignments. Subsequently we integrated the findings in our own coaching practice and developed the Achieve Coaching Model®. The systematic approach has enabled us to achieve consistent and tangible results for and with our clients.

In this part we described each of the seven steps in detail and complemented these descriptions with views from the client perspective and real-life case studies from our international coaching practice:

- **A**ssess the current situation
- **C**reative Brainstorming of alternatives
- **H**one goals
- **I**nitiate options
- **E**valuate options
- **V**alid action programme design
- **E**ncourage momentum

PART FOUR

Using the Achieve Coaching Model® in context

CHAPTER SEVENTEEN The seven core capabilities in context

SEVENTEEN The seven core capabilities in context

Introduction

In parts two and three we described the seven core capabilities of effective executive coaching and detailed a systematic approach for executive coaching assignments with the Achieve Coaching Model®. In this part we provide examples of how the core capabilities are used within the context of the model.

The table below shows the relative importance from our experience of each core capability within the different stages of the Achieve Coaching Model®

	Assess the current situation	Creative brain-storming	Hone goals	Initiate options	Evaluate options	Valid action programme design	Ensure momentum
Rapport building	***	***	***	***	**	***	**
Deep listening	***	***	***	**	**	***	***
Creative questioning	***	***	***	***	**	***	***
Clear goal setting			***			***	
Feedback	**		**	**	**	***	***
Intuition	***	**	**	**	**	**	***
Presence	***	**	**	**	**	**	**

Table 8: The core capabilities

Key: The number of stars indicates relative importance

Assessing the current situation

Our observations and analysis showed that experienced executive coaches are masters of the art of building rapport. The rapport between the executive coach and client is natural and authentic. It is not forced. Rather it is, as one coach described, "... a natural flow that follows awareness." When we observed coaches in action and looked at the physiology of coach and client, those who were most skilled at developing rapport almost looked like they were 'dancing' with the client. In other words, the executive coach and client exhibited similar movements and gestures as though one was leading and the other following.

At this stage it is particularly important to ask genuinely non-judgemental open questions. Any sign of censure from the coach will restrict the executive's willingness to open up.

As an experienced executive coach you have to be constantly aware of your own reactions and how these may impact on your client. When listening to the client we noticed that some less experienced coaches struggled to conceal expressions. In one specific case it became apparent that the coach's facial expressions changed quite markedly when he learned something in the coaching session that did not find his approval. This caused the client to hesitate and hindered his description of the issues he was facing. So, it is essential to suspend your own judgement or at least do not reveal them to your client. Executive coaching is about the client's agenda.

Experienced executive coaches manage to zoom in at critical junctures and ask for a more detailed description and/or information. As one executive coach explained to us, "I am asking questions to help the client begin to really explore his situation. In essence it is this which leads to different ways of thinking about it and ultimately to the self-generation of solutions."

It is also important to let clients talk and provide lots of space. We observed quite marked differences. The more experienced executive coaches appeared to be 'in the situation' and were comfortable with silence and pauses. It is in these silences that the client can be gaining the most valuable insights and can process new ideas. In many ways, to an observer, it can appear that the executive coach is doing very little. The client is doing most of the talking and the work.

We experienced that developing coaches had a tendency to talk more, fill silences with questions and seemed less comfortable with allowing the client to talk uninterrupted. One UK coach admitted that, "At the beginning of my coaching career it was quite a big learning process for me. I had to resist the temptation to speed the process up by cutting in with comments and advice. Now I understand that this indeed hinders the learning process for my client." Another experienced executive coach explained, "I trust the process and know that insights will emerge. It is really critical that I let it happen rather than jumping in and telling stories based on my years of experience in executive positions or providing good advice."

As part of the whole skill of knowing when to remain silent, the ability to listen at a deep level is very important. In our study we noticed that more experienced executive coaches managed to 'switch off' from their own world and are completely there with the client. They applied all their senses to the task of listening, observed their clients very carefully and exhibited a high degree of sensory acuity – an ability to detect physiological changes. Experienced executive coaches also provide signals that they really have been listening by summarizing what has been described. There are three effective techniques we observed:

- **Repeating the exact words**. Experienced executive coaches picked critical words and just repeated them with a rising inflection at the end whilst observing the executive and his reaction.
- **Repeating what has been said by using different words but with the same meaning**. This is more interpretive and aimed at checking mutual understanding.
- **Paraphrasing**. Here some experienced executive coaches went as far as testing emerging working hypotheses and synthesizing information from the client. These experienced executive coaches were very transparent about what they were doing and clearly articulated that they were interpreting what has been said and were formulating a working hypothesis.

What really made us curious is how they managed to really listen after many years in the field where the same patterns, comments or issues by clients may occur over and over again. In other words, how they coped with potential boredom through repetition. The answer is, according to a British coach, really simple: "You genuinely have to be interested in their life stories. If you think 'Here we go again' or 'Oh no, not again' it may be a strong signal to get out of the profession as quickly as your feet can carry you."

The stage of assessing the current situation is certainly an intensive learning phase for both client and executive coach. The skill lies in the art of asking non-judgemental, creative and open questions that invite reflection and talk that, at times, can also include a good moan. In a world where time to talk can feel like the most scarce resource, moaning can be part of the process and can be helpful.

Creative brainstorming of alternatives

Our analysis revealed that experienced coaches ask open and creative questions that aim to surprise and stimulate the client to consider new alternatives that assist in elevating them out of a 'stuck state' or a narrow well-trodden path.

It feels as if the client is standing in front of a huge wall and all he is able to see is two or three bricks. Once you manage to pull the client a bit further away from the wall he gains a wider perspective. In order to master this, an element of surprise and creativity is vital.

One example of this was observed in a session where the client just kept saying "I can't do that." The coach asked, "Well, what would happen if a miracle happened over night and you just did?" This so surprised the client who was used to people accepting her statement that she could not do something that she laughed and then starting producing lists of different ways of approaching her specific challenge.

In addition, the element of rapport needs to be highlighted. It became clear in our study and in our own coaching experience that a careful balance has to be struck between empathy and challenge.

The right application of the core capabilities is in our experience important for establishing an open mindset and to avoid falling into the trap of jumping to solutions which may not be either the best or right for the client.

Honing goals

It is one thing to specify a goal and yet another to ensure that the goal has personal relevance and meaning to the executive. In a business context this can, at times, be forgotten. Most organizations now have a developed performance management system in which individual objectives are defined in terms of the contribution to the organization's overall objectives. Clients may be tempted to use these objectives for the coaching programme. However, we would question whether "increase sales by 15% in the next financial year" has in its current format deep personal relevance for the executive. It is certainly a useful reporting figure for the board and the shareholders but not necessarily that meaningful and relevant for the individual executive. In the coaching programme the executive may feel that it is politically inappropriate to confess that the objectives have little relevance for him.

It is the role of the executive coach, however, to work with the executive to 'translate' the goal into something which really does have meaning for the executive, and one which will still yield the desired result for the organization. As an example, the objective above could be reformulated as: "receive public recognition from the shareholders and board at the next annual meeting for the achievement of the 15% increased sales target."

Skilful use of questioning is again key at this stage. We identified seven areas in which experienced executive coaches use questions to help executives to develop and hone goals:

1. Encourage the executive to state the goal in positive terms.
2. Elicit the specific circumstances in which the coachee wants to achieve the goal. (How does it look/feel? What does he see when he has achieved his goal?)
3. Identify, with the executive, the factors which will indicate that the goal has been achieved.
4. Check ownership of the goal.
5. Check benefits of achievement of the goal on the executive's life.
6. Identify a clear timescale for the achievement of the goal.
7. Check level of commitment for achieving the goal.

It is important that the executive coach listens deeply for statements of goals of real importance and relevance to the executive. In all of this it is crucial that the executive coach does not impose any personal judgements.

Deep listening and checking back with the client is important for the precise formulation of the goal. Remember, it needs to be the executive's goal and not the coach's.

Initiating options

To stimulate the creative process necessary to generate new options it is essential that the coach and executive have built a good level of rapport. Experienced executive coaches told us that they aim to enhance this by working in a comfortable, relaxed environment where everyday concerns and interruptions cannot intrude. This environment should, of course, be present at all times in the coaching process, but at this stage it is of particular relevance and special efforts should be made to ensure a high level of comfort. The executive coach needs to establish with the client what for him are the key elements that will make this the most relaxed and inspiring situation possible, for example, working with the client at a golf club he enjoys.

The skilful use of questions is again vital to the process at this stage. Here the emphasis is on openness and creativity. The characteristics of the questions which elicit the effective generation of new options are as follows:

- **Neutral**. The questions need to be phrased so that no judgement or direction comes through.
- **Probing for breadth instead of depth**. At this stage it is most important that a great variety of options are created.
- **Relational**. Questions encouraging linking past success, may be in an unrelated area to the present situation.
- **Iterative**. Encouraging the executive to build upon previously generated options.
- **"What if ..." questions**. Aiming to unleash creative thought and, in the process, help the executive see that the obstacle is less insurmountable than initially thought and a new option can emerge.

In the initiating options stage the executive coach is listening for statements which may indicate the executive's underlying options – the 'throwaway' statements such as "I could chuck it all in and go to Italy..." which indicate other options which the executive may be self-censoring.

It is important that all options are captured: that is, they are written down on a flip chart, whiteboard or a piece of paper for future reference.

In all coaching sessions we have experienced we noted that one of the great stumbling blocks at this stage of the process is self-censorship. Phrases to watch out for include:

- "We tried this before and failed."
- "It can't be done."
- "If it could be done that way somebody would have done it already."
- "They will never agree to this."
- "I never get the budget for this."
- "I can't afford the time."
- "If it were possible the competition would do it."
- "I am too old for it."

All of these statements contain a negative assertion or are limiting – at times quite severely – potential options. Experienced executive coaches watch out for these and use questions to help the executive overcome them.

These statements tend to be generalizations such as "I always fail." On hearing this type of statement the experienced coach challenges to get at the deep meaning and question the assumptions made by the executive. In the example we experienced that a simple "Always?" with rising inflection stimulated the client to 'defend' himself and then go on to describe a more balanced view from which the coach was able to ask more questions to initiate further options for the client.

Evaluating options

Open questioning styles are once again crucial to allow possibility and to keep the executive stimulated to really think about the consequences of each option. This is a stage where we found ourselves quite often challenged to remain a neutral sparring partner. In the process, the executive coach may have formed his own opinion about the best option for the client and may find it hard to keep it to himself. In addition, clients may choose the easy path and/or seek a decision from the executive coach.

Executive coaches need to be reflective and mindful of the impact of their opinions and actions at this stage. In our experience successful executive coaches ask for permission to voice an opinion or offer advice. If the client agrees, the executive coach can then make a statement but clearly label it for what it is and remind the client of his responsibility for the process.

Questions are used in conjunction with listening to challenge assumptions so that each option is reviewed carefully and not dismissed out of hand. The executive coach also needs to listen for hidden priorities/criteria to ensure that the executive is not limiting his options by falling back to the old well-trodden paths.

Valid action programme design

Open questions at this stage need to be designed with the aim of stimulating the client to formulate clear action steps which will take him towards the achievement of his overall goal. In our study and through our practice we have found that questions such as, "What would be the first small sign of success on the way to achieve the larger goal?" or "What small step could you take over next week which could move you towards your goal?" are useful to move the client forwards and initiate action.

Listening carefully to the client's response helps the executive coach frame the next series of questions and also provides another opportunity for a reality check to ensure the client's commitment to the goals.

Feedback is an essential part of the action plan as at each successive session the executive coach will be enquiring about progress. On the basis of the progress the executive coach will need to provide feedback which is designed to keep the client moving forwards.

In our experience it is highly critical for the overall success of the coaching programme to be able to build momentum with the client so that he begins to make the changes needed to achieve his outcome. It does not matter how big a step forward the client takes. What is important is that some action is taken. As a rule of thumb we work on the assumption in our own practice that the client needs to take a first step within 72 hours of the end of each coaching session to ensure great coaching results and achievement of his goal.

Encourage momentum

Questioning at this stage has the purpose of:

- gathering information about progress
- encouraging the client to keep on track
- affirming positive action and results
- identifying any real or perceived barriers to success

Questions used will be a mixture of open and closed statements such as:

- "How are you getting on with the actions you committed to in the last session?"
- "What positive things have happened since our last session?"
- "What have you changed so far?"
- "What exactly are you doing differently?"
- "How can you build on ...?"
- "What can you do more of ...?"

As the chief role of the executive coach here is to keep the client on track, it is important to consider how to handle situations where the client has made little or no progress. We have found in our own executive coaching practice that a positive focus can be more effective than a deep analysis of barriers and problems and following the "Why not ...?" path.

We were reminded of the importance of a positive focus quite sharply at a recent international coaching convention. One attendee commented to us that, "Creative questions can be used to help refocus the client on the positive actions. Most coaches appear to enjoy dwelling in the mud and, from the supervision I do, I know how easy it is to get lost with the client in the moans, groans and excuses. To my mind this is misplaced empathy."

Thus, while it is important for the executive coach to listen to the client's descriptions of challenges and barriers, the coach should remember that his role is to keep the client moving forwards. Deep listening skills also need to be employed to listen out for small signs of success which can be affirmed and used to stimulate further action. For a successful outcome to the coaching relationship a careful balance needs to be struck between allowing the client to describe what has happened (or not) and injecting further energy and commitment to action.

SUMMARY: THE SEVEN CORE CAPABILITIES IN CONTEXT

This chapter has focused on how the seven core capabilities explored in part two work within the context of the Achieve Coaching Model®.

This chapter has shown how:

- the core capabilities of executive coaching have varying degrees of importance throughout the seven stages of an effective coaching process
- rapport building, creative questioning and listening are key and are used throughout the process
- successful coaching relationships are built using a careful blend and orchestration of all the seven core capabilities

CHAPTER EIGHTEEN Measuring the effectiveness of executive coaching

EIGHTEEN Measuring the effectiveness of executive coaching

Introduction

Decision makers in organizations are increasingly requested by their peers and stakeholders to justify their investments in hiring and deploying executive coaches. With experienced coaches charging around £2000 – £3000 (€2900 – €4500) (in the UK) per day then the costs of a significant coaching programme can be substantial.[4] What tangible returns can be assessed and considered in any business case for coaching? What is the most effective way to track and measure the success of an executive coaching intervention? Is there a foolproof way to provide insights into the return on investment of executive coaching?

Management thinkers, academics and practitioners have struggled with the challenges posed by assessing the benefits of executive coaching, especially those linked to financial benefits. The challenges are similar to the assessment of any other professional service where there are clearly significant intangible as well as tangible benefits discernable. This issue is part of the challenge faced by the Human Resource (Personnel) function and its close sister the Training and Development function. There is no proven magical formula – one size does not fit all. Indeed, it can feel that the evaluation challenge is similar to a request to measure snowflakes before they melt. However, in our experience there are some tried and trusted techniques that can help.

Traditionally it has been difficult to demonstrate an increased value of a company's people (human capital) as a result of many types of HR or training related intervention. Employee costs can make up 40% or more of corporate operating expenses. In some sectors, the lack of precision or rigour behind traditional methods of tracking the return on investment of people-related training interventions has been frustrating.

Footnote: 4 Some executive coaches will base their fees on the basic salary of the client. We have known in-demand coaches charges around 10% of the salary for a six month intervention with senior executives.

It is key to be able to measure the impact of an executive coaching programme so that we can:

- know what the real bottom line impact of executive coaching is
- communicate specific performance expectations convincingly
- provide robust feedback comparing performance to a target or benchmark
- identify performance gaps that need to be eliminated
- recognize performance improvement that should be rewarded
- make decisions regarding resource allocation – failure to be able to do this may result in funds not being made available to support executive coaching if other more convincing business cases have been articulated

Consequently, over the last decade there has been much interest across organizations in concepts such as the balanced scorecard, developed by Robert Kaplan and David Norton from Harvard Business School, in providing frameworks whereby not just standard accounting and finance ratios and measures might be used to judge the performance of an organization.

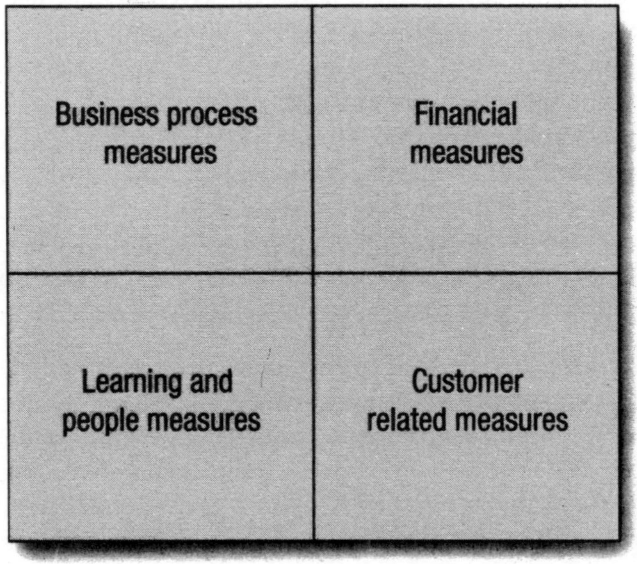

Figure 13: The Balanced scorecard

The scorecard seeks to measure a business from the following perspectives:

- business process perspective
- financial perspective
- customer perspective
- learning and people perspective

The specific measures within each of the perspectives will be chosen to reflect the drivers of the particular business. The balanced scorecard approach marked a significant step forward in that it moved the debate away from just the tracking of financial performance and gave voice to customer and employee learning measures as well.

It is not uncommon to find measures tracked under the 'learning and people' quadrant that include the percentage of managers who have received executive coaching in the last 12 months, or the number of coaching days delivered per manager. But these measures – whilst welcome – tell us little about the impact of executive coaching on organizational improvement of efficiency.

Frequently objectors to applying rigour to measurements of people interventions will be dug in around the myth that only financial or process related information is valid and accurate. As double entry book-keeping practices go back more than 500 years there has built up a belief in organizations about the sanctity of financial statements. In reality the numbers on financial statements (with the possible exception of 'cash in bank') are rarely verifiable as financial truths. Nearly all financial balance sheet numbers are a mix of hope, estimation, best guesses and rounded up expectations. Whilst the conventions that govern the degree of latitude each organization has in estimating and forecasting performance is governed by the expectations of a combination of governing bodies from Her Majesty's Revenue and Customs to the Professional bodies of the Accountancy Profession to the Financial Services Authority.

Consequently, financial balance sheets are good at telling us roughly what has happened historically but the data is only as good as the inputs and the inputs are open to manipulation and interpretation. As a result, there is no reason why similar principles cannot be developed to allow the coaching profession to track the return on the investment made in procuring its services. Indeed, we would argue that this is becoming a requirement for the profession.

Organizations have increasingly become frustrated by the lack of rigor employed by executive coaches in measuring the impact of their work. In our experience, clients are becoming better educated about executive coaching and, whilst they are aware of the technical problems inherent in measuring the organizational impact, they not only require real, clear statistical evidence of the bottom line value of the coaching work but they also need executive coaches to be able to better justify the methodologies they employ. In this chapter we highlight some insights into how the return on investment (ROI) for executive coaching can be measured. However, ROI is not the only tool or measurement approach that should be deployed.

In a recently published report, the UK Chartered Institute of Personnel and Development (CIPD) stressed the importance of attempting to evaluate the tangible benefits of coaching. However, their research concluded that "formal evaluation of coaching initiatives is often lacking, with a large proportion of organizations relying on little more than anecdotal evidence to measure effectiveness"[5].

The survey went on to report that the most common top four measures used to assess the effectiveness of coaching were:

- feedback from participants (used by 75% of organizations surveyed)
- assessment via the annual appraisal system (61%)
- feedback from the coaches (44%)
- employee attitude surveys (41%)

This is not an encouraging picture in terms of robustness of methods deployed. The CIPD also identified that any system of appraisal of coaching should cover:

- the performance of the coach
- feedback concerning the management and administration of the coaching process
- the individual's and line manager's satisfaction with the coaching intervention
- the degree of behaviour change achieved
- the impact on business financial results

Footnote: 5 CIPD (2004), 'Coaching and buying coaching services'.

A four-level model to measuring

These are all important factors but the root of any evaluation of executive coaching should most usefully begin with the approach advocated in 1959 by Don Kirkpatrick. He set out a four-level model of evaluating organizational training. These levels were as follows:

- **Reaction** – measures how those who participate in the programme react to it.
- **Learning** – the extent to which participants change attitudes, improve knowledge, and increase skill as a result of attending the programme.
- **Behaviour** – the extent to which a change in behaviour has occurred because the participants attended the training programme.
- **Results** – the final results that occurred because the participants attended the coaching programme.

Any credible evaluation approach will need to cover these four elements.

1. Measuring reaction

This in our experience is fairly straightforward, although amazingly even this basic level of assessment is missing from many executive coaching programmes.

At the most basic level of measuring reaction to executive coaching, clients can be asked to complete a 'happy sheet' at appropriate points in the programme. Although the nature of the executive coaching process means that the coach is likely to received unsolicited feedback from the client as a matter of course during each session, it is useful to formally collect information of the reaction of the client to the process at the following points:

- after the second coaching session (when the client has had a chance to acclimatize and experience the process)
- at the mid-point in the coaching programme
- at the end of the coaching programme

An example of a simple 'happy sheet' style response form is shown below.

EXAMPLE RESPONSE FEEDBACK FORM

Name of Coach: **Name of Coachee:**

Date & Session no.:

Overall summary

Indicate the degree to which the following qualities were present in the session
(1 = strongly agree, 2 = agree, 3 = neither agree nor disagree, 4 = disagree, 5 = strongly disagree)

I thought we had good rapport	1 2 3 4 5
I felt well listened too	1 2 3 4 5
I felt the coach appropriately probed and challenged me	1 2 3 4 5
I felt that we agreed useful outcomes/goals at the end of each session	1 2 3 4 5
I felt that I received appropriate and constructive feedback	1 2 3 4 5
I have clarified my understanding of the issues I face and the way forward	1 2 3 4 5

General review

What did you find particularly helpful?
What could the coach have done to make it better for you?
What results do you attribute to the coaching process?
Overall on a scale of 1 – 5 (where 1 is outstanding and 5 is very poor) how would you assess the coaching experience to date?

Source: Adapted from the School of Coaching (2004)

At the very least, the executive coach should deploy this type of tool to assess response to the coaching process. Furthermore, probing behind the basic responses that these sheets encourage will often identify particular issues about personal coaching style or process challenges that are impeding the flow of the experience.

2. Measuring learning

Once the initial response factors have been tackled, then the next level of assessment should focus on the extent to which the client achieves the desired change in attitudes, improved knowledge, and increased self-awareness as a result of participating in executive coaching. This is a conceptual minefield as these factors are challenging to both define and track improvements in.

Clients will have a diverse range of learning styles and preferences. People like to learn in different ways whether by reading, interacting with people, or by touching and doing. How people learn from the coaching experience, as much as what they learn, will dictate the approach to measuring that learning.

Furthermore, the outcomes of the coaching experience can be equally diverse. They may include increased knowledge and understanding of self or others around them, development of new skills and abilities or gaining the inspiration to lead more effectively. Learning outcomes can also be short-term and long-term. A client may at times not use his new insights, knowledge or abilities until a long time after the actual coaching session which is a challenge to any assessment or evaluation process.

Measuring learning as an outcome of a coaching relationship is therefore a challenge. It is not surprising that the difficulty of measuring learning in informal environments like executive coaching is continually debated. Added to this is the fact that many of the learning outcomes from executive coaching are so-called 'soft' outcomes. These include attitudes, values, emotions and beliefs which are often critical outcomes that can be altered by the coaching experience. Often these outcomes are not acceptable to organizations as evidence of learning from coaching as the emphasis is on 'hard' facts and demonstrable skills.

Also it would be inappropriate for executive coaches to set specific learning outcomes for clients to achieve. The executive coach does not have prior knowledge of their clients and so would be unable to make judgements about how much clients had learnt. Clients themselves, however, are capable, with some support and guidance, of making such judgements about their own learning.

Although the acquisition of new knowledge or skills might be a side result of the coaching relationship, it is far more likely that the key learning that can be measured will encompass changes in perception about everyday life, expanded knowledge and understanding about the real deep seated issues that have inhibited the growth of fully rounded views of self, family, neighbourhood, or the working world.

3. Measuring skills

Another conceptual challenge is around the concept of measuring improvements in skills. Having a skill means knowing 'how' to do something. There are many different ways that skills can be described. Traditionally organizations have thought of skills as being related to manual ability (e.g. the skills of the welder, electrician, or plumber) or as intellectual skills (e.g. thinking critically and analytically, being able to present a reasoned point of view, numerical competence, weighing up different forms of evidence). From an executive coaching stance the skills that are most likely to be developed are:

- social
- emotional
- communication and
- leadership skills

Social skills

By social we mean enhancing the client's awareness of how his behaviour can impact on others and how developing better social skills, such as boosting the awareness of the importance of building rapport with people, being friendly, introducing others, showing empathy, demonstrating an interest in the concerns of others etc, can lead to an increased understanding of how being more competent at the small social skills can lead to much greater interpersonal influence.

Emotional skills

By emotional skills we mean enhancing the client's ability to manage intense feelings such as anger, being better able to channel energy into productive outcomes, and recognizing and acknowledging the feelings of others. We have observed that small increases in skills in these areas can significantly enhance someone's organizational impact and effectiveness.

Communication skills

By communication skills we mean enhancing writing, speaking, listening, presentational skills, and presenting complex issues in an understandable non-patronizing way.

Leadership skills

By leadership skills we mean the ability of the executive to master his own issues, exhibit leadership in his team, within a project and the organization.

The ability to measure the change in feelings, perceptions, or opinions about self, other people and the team and organization in which the client works is a key element in any executive coaching assessment.

Common outcomes that we have seen in this area include executives developing a much deeper personal understanding, and therefore being able to give reasons for actions and personal viewpoints, increases in empathy, expanded capacity for tolerance and increased feelings of motivation.

4. Measuring attitudes

The changes in social, emotional and communication skills will frequently be the catalyst for changes in attitudes and behaviours. These can be powerful outcomes for the individual and the organization and can lead to dramatic improvements in personal performance at work. Consequently, the process of measuring learning from an executive coaching relationship should focus on:

- attitudes towards self
- attitudes towards others
- attitudes towards the organization

This can manifest itself in changes in the clients' goals at work, or for their careers. It may result in changes in how people balance and manage their lives, including their work, study or family situations. Actions can be observed or clients may self-report what they did and how they perceive their attitude to the world or particular individuals or groups are changing.

We have regularly seen profound changes in the way people manage their professional and personal lives as a result of what they have learned from executive coaching.

One of the best ways to evaluate attitudes is to use a self assessment tool combined with a 360° assessment (involving feedback from, amongst others, peers, managers and direct reports). The most commonly used tools consist of a set of attitudinal statements (e.g. "I often find that I am in the right and others are in the wrong") and then ask for responses about the extent to which the client demonstrates these attitudes at work using a five point scale:

- Almost always
- Often
- Occasionally
- Seldom
- Almost never

It is helpful if attitudes are measured to baseline the individual at the start of the programme and then six months later to track any changes in responses.

Measuring behaviours

The challenges underlying the measurement of behaviour change are similar to those associated with measuring learning or changes in attitudes.

Fundamentally, research from the social science and scientific community indicates that self reported behaviour change is not as reliable a measure as directly observed behaviour change. An everyday example can illustrate this in that individuals will typically over-report seat belt use when compared to actual observations of seat belt use. The same occurrence happens when people are asked to measure their own changes in behaviour as a result of coaching. Individuals will frequently get the trend right (i.e. they will identify that they are doing more of a positive behaviour such as listening to others, and less of a negative behaviour, such as cutting across people and interrupting others) but they will overestimate the degree of change. Possibly this may not matter too much as long as the client is going in the right direction but we have found that the best way to measure behaviour is by use of a 360° tool capturing the views of those around whom the individual interacts with on a day-to-day basis.

However, 360° feedback can be costly and time consuming and in most organizations can realistically only be carried out every 12 to 18 months, so the coach is likely to need to use some form of self assessment tool to allow the client to self-report the changes in behaviour that they are targeting. We have often found that managers will have one or two personal behaviours with which they are extremely dissatisfied. One client was keen to learn to control his temper when he met push-back or disagreement from his fellow workers. By working with the individual to track how often he felt his temper rising we were able to assist him over a two month period to both significantly reduce the occurrence of the undesirable behaviour but also to work to agree and develop better coping strategies to reduce the feelings of anger and frustration.

5. Measuring results

Compared to the issues and challenges with measuring changes in learning, attitudes and behaviours the measurement of results can seem superficially unchallenging. What impact does executive coaching have on the actual business results (top line sales or bottom line profits) of an organization? How can one best capture and assess the benefits against the costs of executive coaching?

Many organizations have been tempted by the old financial measure of Return on Investment (ROI). In our experience less than 10% of organizations use ROI as a tool to assess some aspect of the training and development programmes including executive coaching.

Many executive coaches and clients may be reluctant, however, to use ROI where the outcomes may be hard to quantify. We have found that the ROI approach to measuring results is a viable approach when combined with the application of a little common sense and an understanding of the limitations of it as a measurement tool.

The classic definition of ROI is earnings divided by the investment – no matter what the application. In the context of calculating the return on investment in executive coaching, the earnings become the net benefits from the programme (monetary benefits minus the costs), and the investment is the actual programme cost (plus opportunity costs if work time is taken). The difficulty lies is identifying what the actual monetary benefits attributable to executive coaching are in a credible way.

We are not, of course, advocating that the executive coaching programme's value can be reduced to the simplicities of one ROI number. The data and measures driven out from the process of measuring the response and changes in learning, attitudes and behaviours, explored above, are fundamental and need to be given full consideration.

ROI is a useful measure for expressing the consequence of the executive coaching programme in monetary terms. For organizations with a culture welded to the financial mindset of investment and return, it can be useful to adopt the ROI approach to engage with senior stakeholders in terms they are comfortable with and knowledgeable about. This is especially so if the assumptions behind the ROI calculations are transparent and understood: ROI then becomes a useful measure for assessing the effectiveness of executive coaching within an organization.

Of course, the issue with executive coaching ROI is that its calculations can easily be based on nothing but estimates that are very subjective. When estimating ROI there are usually four areas where subjective errors can creep in:

- the degree of improvement in performance is estimated when records are not readily available to show the improvement
- the top and bottom line effects of the programme are not easy to disentangle from other initiatives, the impact of other individuals or the wider fluctuations in market conditions
- when converting outputs into monetary values
- the basic assumptions used to calculate the costs of the executive coaching programme

One of the key challenges with ROI is avoiding too complicated an approach. The ROI calculation itself is a simple ratio: benefits divided by costs. Guiding principles need to be developed which clearly show the assumptions about what can and cannot be included as a benefit or cost. This is a potential minefield because all the different situations, programmes and projects in which an individual is involved will need to be evaluated.

For most clients it is a challenge to isolate the effects of their executive coaching programme from other organizational factors. This is the most difficult and challenging issue, but it is always possible, even if estimates are used, to derive some set of numbers. Of course when estimates are used these should be clearly identified and any accompanying assumptions spelled out.

Another key decision is to decide whether using the ROI approach is appropriate for every executive coaching programme. In practice it is often not feasible for all coaching interventions to be subject to ROI evaluation. Ideally only those executive coaching programmes that are very expensive, strategically important or highly visible within the organization should be included.

In our experience, at present less than 10% of executive coaching programmes are subject to an ROI analysis. However, this number is set to increase. ROI analysis is particularly useful if the whole of the management team have been through a programme – in this situation the overall executive coaching programme (rather than an individual managerial event) can be analyzed.

Ideally when conducting the ROI study the person evaluating the programme should be independent of the programme (i.e. not an executive coach or client). It is important for the stakeholders to understand that the person conducting the study is objective and removed from certain parts of the study, such as the data collection and the initial analysis. Sometimes these issues can be addressed in a partnering role or limited in outsourcing opportunities – whether data collection or analysis. In other situations, the issue must be addressed and the audience must understand that steps are taken to ensure that the data are collected objectively, analyzed and reported completely.

How to calculate the ROI from a coaching programme

ROI analysis is best undertaken at the end of the agreed executive coaching programme. Typically, a mix of qualitative and quantitative data is collected from the client(s) and his/their employer. On the whole, we have found that the following questions for clients are useful:[6]

1. Looking back over the programme, please describe the performance improvement that you have realized as a result of the executive coaching. In your answer you may wish to include reference to internal documents such as performance and development reviews and appraisals.
2. What impact do these improvements have on the organization? Please tick as appropriate.
   - Increased output/sales
   - Increased personal productivity
   - Increased team productivity
   - Increased product quality
   - Improved customer relationships
   - Reduced customer complaints
   - Reduction in delivery times
   - Other (please specify)

(These questions should, of course, be modified according to the nature of the client organization.)

Footnote: 6 The questions are inspired by the pre conference session at the International Coach Federation Conference 2003 'Measuring magic: applying ROI strategies to coaching' Metrixglobal, LLC

3. For each item that the client has ticked above he then needs to complete a benefit calculation using the following table:

Indicator of impact	Estimated annual monetary value of performance improvement	Percentage improvement due to coaching	Percentage confidence in this estimate	Value
Introduction of a web based system to report orders	£25,000	100%	75%	£18,750
Increased ability to set motivating sales targets for team	£235,000	50%	75%	£88,125
Reduced meeting time	£30,000	80%	60%	£14,400
Introduction of a new incentive system	£180,000	100%	80%	£144,000
TOTAL				**£265,275**

Table 9: Benefit calculation

4. When the table is as complete as possible for all items, the monetary benefit can be calculated with the following formula:

   Monetary value =
   Estimated annual monetary value of performance improvement
   x Estimated percentage improvement due to coaching
   x Percentage confidence in this estimate.

An overall sum is produced when these calculations are then added up. This figure and the supporting calculations are then passed to the executive coach who then works with the programme sponsors to validate the assessments. It is useful during this rather mechanistic process to get the client to also note down the 'intangible benefits' of the executive coaching programme (i.e. greater self awareness, more confidence, greater sense of self worth) as these should not be forgotten.

In the example shown above (Table 9) the client had identified four monetary impacts from participating in coaching. The first gives a weighted value of £18,750 ((£25,000 x 1) x .75) and the second equates to £88,125 ((£235,000 x .5) x .75). After all four benefits have been calculated the overall benefit identified from coaching is £265,275.

The issue with this calculation is, of course, the estimation of the 'improvement' and 'confidence' percentages. In the example the manager estimated that 75% of the benefits due to the introduction of a web based order reporting system was due to coaching. We have found that experienced managers are normally able to make educated estimates around these percentage figures, and the process whereby they formulate these estimates in discussion with the executive coach is a useful exercise in itself.

5. Once the monetary benefit has been calculated the executive coach is required to determine the cost of the coaching engagement. This normally needs the following items to be included:
   - professional fees charged
   - the opportunity costs of the client's time to participate in the coaching sessions
   - the costs of materials used (meeting rooms, external assessment tools/surveys etc)
   - travel expenses
   - administration costs

The executive coach adds all the costs to produce a total figure. These costs also need validating with the programme sponsors to ensure consistency and accuracy. Once this is done then the simple maths of calculating the ROI of coaching can be completed, namely:

Calculate Return on Coaching Investment =

ROI = ((Benefits – Costs) / Cost) x 100

So, if the benefits had been identified as being £265,275 and the costs as being £35,000 then the calculation is:

ROI = ((265,275 – 35,000) / 35,000) x 100 = 658%

This is an impressive figure indicating that each £1 invested in coaching has generated more than £6 of increased output. This number can be used most effectively in the executive coach's final report on the programme to the stakeholders and sponsors. Indeed, research in the US by Lore International in 2004 has demonstrated that the ROI of an executive coaching programme with an experienced coach is on average in the region of 600%-1000%.

The seven critical success factors for demonstrating ROI from executive coaching

In our experience there are seven critical success factors for demonstrating the ROI of executive coaching. These are listed below:

1. Begin by setting objectives for the executive coaching session according to SMART principles (specific, measurable, achievable, realistic and time bound) and establish a benchmark for performance from existing appraisals and reviews.
2. Ensure that the executive coaching objectives flow from overall project objectives and/or business objectives.
3. Communicate the methodology for measuring the monetary value of the executive coaching programme before the programme begins.
4. Check with internal experts within the organization (e.g. HR or finance managers) for critical figures and assumptions to use (e.g. opportunity costs client time for participating in coaching and other assumptions that the client may have set in stone for use in calculating an ROI approach).
5. Capture the monetary value of the executive coaching in tandem with the intangible value. This typically requires the use of some of the tools and approaches we have identified under the initial response, learning, attitudes and behaviours' sections of this chapter.
6. Validate your calculations and assumptions with the client, the sponsor and other key stakeholders to ensure buy-in to the figures being generated.
7. Communicate the results of the executive coaching programme to key stakeholders in the organization.

Table 10: The seven critical success factors for demonstrating the ROI of executive coaching

For the coaching profession as a whole, demonstrating ROI using a clear well-defined methodology will assist in raising the profile of the profession as being responsible and accountable, as well as contributing to the recognition of coaching as a critical and valuable tool for organizational development. Calculating the ROI of executive coaching is not an easy process but when implemented alongside the other assessment approaches discussed in this chapter, it does create a robust and defendable set of data to judge the effectiveness of executive coaching programmes.

Matching tools to the need to evaluate

The table below summarizes our experience of the best tools or elements to use for each different level of evaluation. Obviously not every organization can afford to invest the time and effort required to measure all aspects of the impact of executive coaching. At the very least, however, organizations should look to use some form of tool to collect the reaction of the client to the programme, the individual's line manager's satisfaction with the outcomes, and to assess the achievements of the objectives agreed at the start of the coaching relationship.

	Measuring Reaction	Measuring Learning and Attitude	Measuring Behaviours	Measuring Results
Individual satisfaction with coaching (via 'happy sheet' collection)	✔✔	✔	✔	✗
Client's Line Manager's assessment of impact of coaching	✔	✔✔	✔✔	✔
Employee attitude / climate surveys	✗	✔	✔	✗
The performance of the executive coach as rated by clients	✔✔	✗	✗	✗
Staff turnover rates / improved retention rates	✗	✗	✔	✔
Feedback from the executive coach	✔✔	✔	✔	✗
Achievement of objectives agreed at the start of the programme	✔	✔	✔	✔
Comparison on pre/post coaching 360º ratings	✔	✔✔	✔✔	✗
Impact on business performance via ROI assessment	✗	✗	✗	✔✔
Improved appraisal / performance ratings	✗	✔	✔	✔✔
Self assessment psychometric instruments	✗	✔✔	✔✔	✗

✔✔ High ✔ Medium ✗ Low

Table 11: The best tools or elements for evaluation of executive coaching

SUMMARY: MEASURING THE EFFECTIVENESS OF EXECUTIVE COACHING

Measuring the impact of executive coaching is important but difficult. Frequently organizations make little attempt at applying any rigor to measuring the outcomes. The coach and the organization should aim to capture data and measures the impact at four levels:

- reaction
- learning
- behaviour
- business results

This chapter has highlighted a number of tools and approaches at each of these four levels.

Calculating the ROI, so that the financial impact of the executive coaching intervention may be estimated is possible and the process by which it can be calculated is a useful exercise in itself. Research in the US shows that the return on executive coaching typically falls into an impressive 600% – 1000%. Therefore each £1 spent on coaching can generate between £6 and £10 back. This is an attractive investment provided that the right experienced executive coach is selected, and clear goals and objectives are set.

Measuring the results of executive coaching is a challenge but good executive coaches are increasingly realizing that it is a necessity rather than a luxury, if boardroom attention and credibility is to be won.

Top tips include:

- make sure that some element of evaluation occurs even if you cannot convince the client to go as far as calculating the ROI
- measuring the reaction to learning is simple and straightforward, and should always be undertaken as part of being a professional executive coach
- develop examples of how to measure executive coaching that you can use in your business development discussions
- do not be afraid of evaluation. Business people are used to quantifying their activities and outputs, and by adopting a similar approach you will be talking their language

CHAPTER NINETEEN Future trends and outlook

NINETEEN Future trends and outlook

Introduction

In the preceding chapters we have examined the core capabilities and the hallmarks of excellence in executive coaching. We have provided a clear systematic approach which can be used to structure both individual coaching sessions and an overall coaching programme.

Now we turn our focus to the future: what are the trends in executive coaching?

The developments we cover are derived both from thought leaders[7] in the coaching profession and our own views.

We focus on seven key trends:

- Development of professional standards
- Increased professionalization of the service
- Development of organizational coaching cultures
- Growth of internal coaching activities
- Multiple tiers in executive coaching provision – the growth of differentiation
- Method integration
- Growth in group coaching activities

Development of professional standards

There are various factors fuelling the development of professional standards for executive coaching. At this stage 'executive coach' is a title which anyone can use to describe themselves and their professional service offering. Unlike other professional services, such as accountancy or law,

Footnote: 7 Special thanks are due to: Prof. David Clutterbuck, Prof. David Lane, Sir John Whitmore and Wendy Johnson there are very few barriers to entry and no formal requirements for training or accreditation before you can describe yourself as an executive coach. While this is common in the developmental stage of a profession, it does lead to confusion.

Organizational buyers of executive coaching services and private clients are confused by the use of the term and the multiplicity of business and executive coaches. With no clear professional qualifications and standards, the buyers of coaching services lack guidance about whose services to use. In addition, although low barriers to entry make for an inclusive profession, the lack of defined standards can create problems for the acceptance of the profession as a whole.

Concern for this lack of acceptance, a need for clarity and the development of a robust profession has led the various professional bodies around the world, for example, ICF, WABC and EMCC, to begin the process of developing competencies and standards. In addition, national training organizations, universities and other accrediting bodies are setting standards for coach training.

The challenge will be to gain agreement about the standards as no one single body represents the whole coaching profession. Each organization exists to serve the interests of its own members. Gradually a consensus needs to be reached, however, and the existence of standards and recognized qualifications will provide greater transparency for the users of executive coaching services and provide a more solid foundation for the coaching profession.

There is a stage in the development of any profession where different groups representing different interests see a common value in cooperation and overcome the differences for the common good. In coaching this is beginning, at the time of going to press, but not yet achieved.

Increased professionalization of the service

Coupled with the drive towards common standards and competencies in executive coaching, it is evident in the market place that there is an increased professionalization of the organizations and individuals providing coaching services. This move towards professional practices seen in other professions such as psychology, accountancy and management consultancy is exemplified by such factors as formal contracts setting out roles and responsibilities and clarifying expectations about intended outcomes, well-produced marketing materials, intellectual debate in academic and professional journals, and an emphasis on the experience and qualifications of the individual executive coaches. It is an indicator of the burgeoning growth of the profession and also the increasing demands placed on executive coaches by their client organizations. These demands are as high as in any other professional service.

A profession builds on a common platform of expertise: agreement on that common platform marks the point at which a profession can lay claim to expert status. To claim that status, however, also requires acceptance of that status by the public and client organizations. Executive coaching organizations and coaches cannot just claim professional status – they must find common understanding with their potential clients.

Development of organizational coaching cultures

The use of executive coaching for individuals within the organization is on the increase – recent surveys conducted by The School of Coaching and the Chartered Institute for Personnel and Development in the UK indicate that between 92% and 97% of organizations use coaching services.

However, only a few organizations are fully committed to developing a coaching culture to create a new way of management. Some pioneers have adopted this new style but many others are still struggling to find ways of moving away from old command and control management habits.

The benefits of initiating a coaching culture are many and are in line with the trends towards flatter organizational structures. The benefits include creating a more open and honest climate where issues can be discussed, increased perception of organizational commitment to individual development and career advancement, a more rapid spread of behaviours which support organizational values and a decrease in expenditure on external support.

However, introducing a coaching culture to any organization brings the same challenges as other culture change programmes. It is not sufficient merely to announce it, provide information and assume that the change will take place. As with any culture change, planning is essential to introduce the new initiative. With an increase in the size of the organization the challenge will grow. International, cross-cultural and diversity aspects will receive increasing emphasis and are an integral part of developing a sound coaching culture.

It is important to examine all the costs and benefits, and to anticipate and plan for resistance. We anticipate that the trend towards the development of coaching cultures within organizations will continue to increase.

Growth of internal coaching activities

As the use of executive coaching as a personal development service has spread, those in control of budgets within organizations have drawn attention to the increased spend on coaching activities. This has caused some large, leading organizations to develop their own internal coaching capabilities. Generally this is led by a small team within the Human Resources department who undertake a programme to develop internal coaches. The internal coaches receive varying degrees of training and supervision. In leading organizations we have observed two main types of programmes. In some, individuals take on coaching responsibilities in addition to their existing day-to-day activities. This may take the format of more experienced individuals providing coaching outside of the normal line management structure or the provision of coaching services to colleagues across the organization.

In other programmes, individuals are trained as coaches and then devote all their time to providing coaching across the organization and, in some cases, to other external organizations. In this way the organization develops an entirely separate coaching service.

Internal coaching activities are perceived to be a cost effective option for organizations especially for lower and middle management levels, and hence this is a trend which is set to spread more widely. Internal coaching services tend not to reach upper management levels and the boardroom. For those external coaches operating at middle and lower management levels this trend presents a potential threat to market share, business growth and puts pressure on fees. However, within organizations most strongly committed to coaching culture there is also a trend to use external coaches as trainers and supervisors of the internal coaches – this is an emerging area of business.

Multiple tiers in executive coaching provision – the growth of differentiation

As mentioned above, the development of internal coaching capabilities within organizations is beginning to have an impact on the market place. This, combined with an increasing number of coaching service providers, puts pressure on the level of fees that can be charged for coaching at lower and middle management levels.

Under the influence of these market pressures there are distinct signs of a trend towards developing services that are differentiated according to the level of the individual being coached. In particular there is a small premium market emerging to service those at the highest levels within an organization.

For this group it is particularly important that executive coaching providers market their full profile including such things as their coaches' educational level, past experiences in blue chip organizations, leadership roles in business or sports, and any distinct intellectual capital in the area of executive coaching and leadership services. By matching the profile of the company to those it seeks to coach, coaching providers can deliver a differentiated service which gives them a competitive advantage and offers the client benefits which they cannot obtain elsewhere. The service offering has to be pitched at the level of the client or to the level to which he aspires.

This trend echoes the developments seen in other services which have grown in popularity and acceptance.

Method integration

The market and individual sectors have become more sophisticated in their demands of coaching providers. Whereas in the past it may have been sufficient to be able to operate within one field of expertise based on techniques such as Neuro Linguistic Programming (NLP), Gestalt or Transactional Analysis there is a marked trend towards a demand for a greater breadth of techniques, experience and training. This is exemplified by the inclusion of elements of transpersonal psychology, spiral dynamics, psychosynthesis and the integrated approach of thinkers such as Ken Wilber into coach training programmes.

All of these newer approaches aim to provide the executive coach with more resources with which to work with clients on developing meaning and purpose within their professional and personal lives.

Executive coaches that operate in the premium segment of the market usually undertake a number of coach training programmes and understand a variety of methods and techniques. Increasingly there is an integration of the various methods and techniques which equip the executive coach to work with a diversity of clients and situations. By broadening their technical repertoire the executive coach is also able to achieve measurable and sustainable results with the client within a short space of time.

This trend is reflected in the executive coach training field where course content is increasingly derived from multiple disciplines to produce multifaceted practitioners with a breadth of techniques in their toolkit.

This trend is also reflected in coaches' supervision arrangements where, for example, coaches with a psychology background purposefully choose a supervisor from the business world and vice versa, or where an NLP trained executive coach chooses a supervisor trained in Gestalt. We regard this as an increasingly valid path to ensure further method integration and see it as a great contribution to strengthening the knowledge base within the profession.

Growth in group coaching activities

Although much of the focus in executive coaching is centred on the individual, we have noted a growth in group coaching activities. In general this is aimed at top team development and is usually a combination of group and individual activity. The individual sessions are used to complement the group activity by reinforcing learning and allowing time for individual development of core skills and behaviours. As well as using individual coaching to complement group activity, the whole group is sometimes coached together.

Coaching whole groups requires an executive coach to have well developed facilitation skills and an ability to differentiate the approach to meet the needs of all of the individuals within the group. The challenge for executive coaches will be to master the dynamics of the different degrees of openness from different members of the group. Working with groups will also reveal different aspects of an organization than in the individual coaching work. This needs to be handled with care and issues of information sharing need to be discussed with individual clients before entering a group coaching situation.

This trend is likely to spread as it is viewed as a more cost-effective method of providing coaching to the senior team and has the additional benefit of increasing communication and effective working practices amongst senior team members. In addition, and perhaps most importantly, the growth in group coaching strengthens the whole coaching process within an organization. A greater dynamic within an organization can be created and real changes on an organizational level can be achieved through group working.

The true opportunity in the future of executive coaching is not what it does to make businesses more successful, but, as Wendy Johnson points out, the influence it has on a 'bigger life' picture. As business coaching becomes more prevalent in global organizations, coaches will challenge and support individuals within those organizations to stay true to their personal values, ethics and morals. The opportunity then for executive coaching to influence beyond the immediate sphere of the client and the organization begins to gain momentum as more and more individuals are inspired to act upon their guiding principles.

What does this mean for the future of executive coaching? It means the following:

- **More focus on ethics**: Global organizations are operating at a speed of change that exceeds the speed of regulation. This gap creates an environment of self-regulation that often challenges ethical and moral boundaries. Executive coaches in the future can expect clients to struggle with even more ethical and moral decisions.
- **More focus on balance**: Technology will continue to make virtual operations easier and more flexible. However, global business requires communication over a variety of time zones. Psychologists and family therapists cite wireless technology and being "constantly connected to the office" as leading causes of marriage and family distress. Executive coaches in the future can expect clients to search for more personal and professional balance while operating in a 24/7 world.

Executive coaching in the future will not only support individuals who will in turn build up their businesses, but also support individuals who will in turn work on a broader stage ... creating worldwide influence.

SUMMARY: FUTURE TRENDS AND OUTLOOK

This chapter has focused on the trends that may drive the market and the profession of coaching for the foreseeable future.

The trends identified include:

- development of professional standards for executive coaches
- increased professionalization of the service
- development of organizational coaching cultures
- growth of internal coaching activities
- growth of differentiation in executive coaching
- pressures to achieve method integration
- growth in demand for group coaching

Overall, we concluded that these trends will drive an increased focus on ethical aspects to executive coaching discussions and even more desire by clients to achieve a better balance between their personal and professional lives.

Further reading and organizations

Further reading and organizations

Bacon, T and Spear, K I (2003), *Adaptive Coaching: The Art and Practice of a Client-Centered Approach to Performance Improvement*, Davies-Black Publishing

Beck, D and Cowan, C (2005), *Spiral Dynamics: Mastering Values, Leadership and Change*, Blackwell

Caplan, J (2002), *Coaching for the Future: How Smart Companies use Coaching and Mentoring*, CIPD

Clutterbuck, D and Megginson, D (2004), *Techniques for Coaching and Mentoring*, Butterworth-Heinemann

Clutterbuck, D and Megginson, D (2005), *Making Coaching Work: Creating a Coaching Culture*, CIPD

Downey, M (1999), *Effective Coaching*, Orion Business Books

Flaherty, J (1998), *Coaching: Evoking Excellence in Others*, Butterworth-Heinemann

Gallwey, T (2000), *The Inner Game of Work*, Orion Business Books

Goldsmith, M and Lyons, L (Eds) (2000), *Coaching for Leadership: How the World's Greatest Coaches Help Leaders Learn*, Jossey Bass Wiley

Greene, J and Grant, A M (2003), *Solution-focused Coaching: Managing People in a Complex World*, Momentum

Landsberg, M (1996), *The Tao of Coaching*, Harper Collins Business

McDermott, I and Jago, W (2005), *The Coaching Bible: The Complete Guide to Developing Personal and Professional Effectiveness*, Piatkus

McFadzean, E.S (1999), *Creativity in MS/OR: Choosing the Appropriate Technique*, Interfaces, Vol.29 No.5, pp 110-22

Parsloe, E (1999), *The Manager as Coach and Mentor (2nd Edition)*, CIPD

Rosinski, P. (2003), *Coaching Across Cultures,* Nicholas Brealey Publishing

Schmidt-Tanger, M (1999), Veränderungscoaching Kompetent verandern, Junfermann

Starr, J (2002), *The Coaching Manual: The Definitive Guide to the Process and Skills of Personal Coaching,* Prentice Hall

Wilber, K (2001), *A Theory of Everything: An Integral Vision for Business, Politics, Science and Spirituality,* Gateway

Whitmore, J (2002), *Coaching for Performance: Growing People, Performance and Purpose,* Nicholas Brealey Publishing Ltd.

Whitworth, L et al. (1998), *Co-active Coaching: New Skills for Coaching People Toward Success in Work and Life,* Davies-Black Publishing

Zeus, P and Skiffington, S (2000), *The Complete Guide to Coaching at Work,* McGraw Hill

Organizations

Deutscher Bundesverband Coaching
www.dbvc.de

European Mentoring and Coaching Council
www.emccouncil.org

International Coaching Federation
www.coachfederation.org

The Coaching and Mentoring Network
www.coachingnetwork.org.uk

The European Coaching Association e.V.
www.eca-online.de

Worldwide Association of Business Coaches
www.wabccoaches.com

Training courses

Achieve Coaching Model® Training
For further information contact:

Dr Sabine Dembkowski
Sabinedembkowski@thecoachingcentre.com
Telephone: +44 (0)20 8374 2877 or +49 (0)221 285 9605

Your comments

We are most interested in your feedback. Please do not hesitate to contact us: sabinedembkowski@thecoachingcentre.com

Appendices

Appendices

Appendix 1: Definitions of coaching

Definition	Author
Developing a person's skills and knowledge so that their job performance improves, hopefully leading to the achievement of organizational objectives. It targets high performance and improvement at work, although it may also have an impact on an individual's private life. It usually lasts for a short period and focuses on specific skills and goals.	CIPD (2004)
Primarily a short-term intervention aimed at performance improvement or developing a particular competence.	Clutterbuck (2003)
A conversation, or series of conversations, one person has with another.	Starr (2003)
A coach is a collaborative partner who works with the learner to help them achieve goals, solve problems, learn and develop.	Caplan (2003)
A process that enables learning and development to occur and thus performance to improve.	Parsloe (1999)
The art of facilitating the performance, learning and development of another.	Downey (1999)
Unlocking a person's potential to maximize their own performance.	Whitmore (1996)

Table 12: Definitions of coaching

Appendix 2: Commonly used psychometric instruments

Psychometric Instrument	Explanation
Verbal Reasoning	This assesses an individual's ability to accurately extract key information from written information and make reasoned judgements under the pressure of time. The test contains several passages of text and the individual is required to extract pertinent information from the texts in order to answer a series of questions. The test is timed.
Numerical Reasoning	This test is designed to assess the ability to manipulate complex numeric and financial data. It gives an indication of how effectively someone will manage financial information at work. This test allows the use of a calculator and is timed.
Abstract Reasoning	This taps into an individual's ability to think conceptually, identify key issues in complex information and is often linked to speed of learning. The test contains a series of abstract patterns and explores an individual's ability to adopt a flexible, lateral approach to problem solving when faced with unfamiliar information. It is useful for roles that contain a strong strategic element. This test is timed.
Motivation Questionnaire	Performance is a combination of motivation and ability – in order to be successful, an individual has to be driven to use their talent effectively. This questionnaire explores what characteristics of a role are likely to motivate an individual and therefore where they are likely to invest most of their energy. This is an untimed, self-report questionnaire.
Business Challenges	The Andrews Munro Business Challenges questionnaire indicates how leaders view the world of work, and identifies their preferences in tackling strategic challenges. For example, some may be inclined to focus on sound financial management as a strategy for success, whereas others may place greater emphasis on representing an organization's interest in the external community. This is an untimed self-report questionnaire.

Career Tactics	The Andrews Munro Career Tactics questionnaire helps senior level individuals and organizations understand the organizational realities of career success and failure. It can identify which tactics individuals tend to deploy – which are 'winning', which are 'constraints' and which may be 'downfall' tactics. A useful tool to open a dialogue to help maximize personal effectiveness. This is an untimed, self-report questionnaire.
Conflict Mode Questionnaire	The Thomas-Kilmann Conflict Mode Instrument looks at an individual's typical approach to handling conflict. It provides a profile based on five styles (accommodating, avoiding, collaborating, competing and compromizing), positioned along two dimensions (assertiveness and cooperativeness). This is a short, untimed self-report questionnaire.
Firo-B	The Fundamental Interpersonal Relations Orientation-Behaviour questionnaire measures how an individual typically behaves towards others and also how that individual would like others to behave towards them. It is very useful for development purposes. It is an untimed self-report questionnaire.
OPQ Personality Profile	This questionnaire gives an indication of how someone is likely to operate in the workplace and provides insights into a range of leadership competencies. It has been shown to have a strong predictive validity. It is an untimed self-report questionnaire.
MBTI	The Myers-Briggs Type Indicator classifies individuals according to a range of psychological types. These classifications indicate where people prefer to focus their attention, how they gather information, the way they make decisions and how they deal with the outside world. This is an untimed self-report questionnaire.

Table 13: Common psychometric instruments and their uses

Appendix 3: The development of coaching – background influences

We have found that individual coaches had an enormous variety of backgrounds and educational profiles. For example, in Germany most coaches have a strong psychological or therapeutic background, whereas in the US and UK most executive coaches have been in senior positions in the private or public sector and have undertaken further training in one or more of the fields influencing coaching practice. The diversity adds to the richness of experience and capability of the profession but also complicates the attempts by leading organizations such as the European Mentoring and Coaching Council (EMCC), the International Coach Federation (ICF) and the Worldwide Association of Business Coaches (WABC) to define best practice and establish standards. In the UK, national standards are being compiled by ENTO (an independent standards setting body committed to developing the competence of people who work with people) which will govern vocational qualifications and training but will still focus on outputs, rather than prescribe the background of the coach.

It is beyond the scope of this book to provide a detailed examination of each of the major influential fields impacting on the development of coaching practice. However, the main influences are listed below and some suggestions for further reading are provided earlier in this book.

FIELD	EXAMPLES OF AUTHORS
Creativity	Gardner
Psychology	Wilber
Personal development	Chopra, Robbins, Redfield
Emotional intelligence	Goleman
Learning theory	Kolb, McCarthy
Thinking skills	De Bono, Buzan
Sports psychology	Galwey, Garfield
Motivation theory	McClelland, Locke
Communication theory including NLP	Bandler, Grinder, James, Dilts

FIELD	EXAMPLES OF AUTHORS
Systems thinking	Senge
Management development	Blanchard, Covey,
Appreciative inquiry	Cooperrider
Spiral Dynamics	Graves, Beck and Cowan
Psychosynthesis	Assagioli, Whitmore, D

Table 14: Background influences

Whatever the background of the coach and the influences on their training and development, it has become clear to us through our study and practice of executive coaching that a structured approach to the process is pivotal to the development of the profession and standards.